CANCER

THE ENCYCLOPEDIA OF

H E A L T H

MEDICAL DISORDERS
AND THEIR TREATMENT

Dale C. Garell, M.D. · General Editor

CANCER

Joann Ellison Rodgers

Introduction by C. Everett Koop, M.D., Sc.D.
Surgeon General, U.S. Public Health Service

CHELSEA HOUSE PUBLISHERS
New York · Philadelphia

The goal of the ENCYCLOPEDIA OF HEALTH *is to provide general information in the ever-changing areas of physiology, psychology, and related medical issues. The titles in this series are not intended to take the place of the professional advice of a physician or other health-care professional.*

ON THE COVER False-Color Scanning Electron Micrograph of a T-Lymphocyte Killer
    Cell Attacking a Large Cancer Tumor Cell

Chelsea House Publishers
EDITOR-IN-CHIEF Nancy Toff
EXECUTIVE EDITOR Remmel T. Nunn
MANAGING EDITOR Karyn Gullen Browne
COPY CHIEF Juliann Barbato
PICTURE EDITOR Adrian G. Allen
ART DIRECTOR Maria Epes
MANUFACTURING MANAGER Gerald Levine

The Encyclopedia of Health
SENIOR EDITOR Paula Edelson

Staff for CANCER
ASSOCIATE EDITOR Will Broaddus
COPY EDITOR Mark Rifkin
EDITORIAL ASSISTANT Leigh Hope Wood
PICTURE RESEARCHER Georganne Backman
ASSISTANT ART DIRECTOR Loraine Machlin
SENIOR DESIGNER Marjorie Zaum
DESIGN ASSISTANT Debora Smith
PRODUCTION MANAGER Joseph Romano
PRODUCTION COORDINATOR Marie Claire Cebrián

3 5 7 9 8 6 4

Library of Congress Cataloging-in-Publication Data

Rodgers, Joann Ellison.
  Cancer/Joann Rodgers; introduction by C. Everett Koop.
    p. cm.—(The Encyclopedia of health. Medical disorders and their treatment)
  Includes bibliographical references.
  ISBN 0-7910-0059-1.
      0-7910-0486-4 (pbk.)
  1. Cancer—Popular works. I. Title. II. Series.
RC263.R632 1990   89-17417
616.99'4—dc 20   CIP

CONTENTS

THE ENCYCLOPEDIA OF
H E A L T H

THE HEALTHY BODY

The Circulatory System
Dental Health
The Digestive System
The Endocrine System
Exercise
Genetics & Heredity
The Human Body: An Overview
Hygiene
The Immune System
Memory & Learning
The Musculoskeletal System
The Neurological System
Nutrition
The Reproductive System
The Respiratory System
The Senses
Speech & Hearing
Sports Medicine
Vision
Vitamins & Minerals

THE LIFE CYCLE

Adolescence
Adulthood
Aging
Childhood
Death & Dying
The Family
Friendship & Love
Pregnancy & Birth

MEDICAL ISSUES

Careers in Health Care
Environmental Health
Folk Medicine
Health Care Delivery
Holistic Medicine
Medical Ethics
Medical Fakes & Frauds
Medical Technology
Medicine & the Law
Occupational Health
Public Health

PSYCHOLOGICAL DISORDERS AND THEIR TREATMENT

Anxiety & Phobias
Child Abuse
Compulsive Behavior
Delinquency & Criminal Behavior
Depression
Diagnosing & Treating Mental Illness
Eating Habits & Disorders
Learning Disabilities
Mental Retardation
Personality Disorders
Schizophrenia
Stress Management
Suicide

MEDICAL DISORDERS AND THEIR TREATMENT

AIDS
Allergies
Alzheimer's Disease
Arthritis
Birth Defects
Cancer
The Common Cold
Diabetes
First Aid & Emergency Medicine
Gynecological Disorders
Headaches
The Hospital
Kidney Disorders
Medical Diagnosis
The Mind-Body Connection
Mononucleosis and Other Infectious Diseases
Nuclear Medicine
Organ Transplants
Pain
Physical Handicaps
Poisons & Toxins
Prescription & OTC Drugs
Sexually Transmitted Diseases
Skin Disorders
Stroke & Heart Disease
Substance Abuse
Tropical Medicine

PREVENTION AND EDUCATION: THE KEYS TO GOOD HEALTH

C. Everett Koop, M.D., Sc.D.
Surgeon General,
U.S. Public Health Service

The issue of health education has received particular attention in recent years because of the presence of AIDS in the news. But our response to this particular tragedy points up a number of broader issues that doctors, public health officials, educators, and the public face. In particular, it points up the necessity for sound health education for citizens of all ages.

Over the past 25 years this country has been able to bring about dramatic declines in the death rates for heart disease, stroke, accidents, and, for people under the age of 45, cancer. Today, Americans generally eat better and take better care of themselves than ever before. Thus, with the help of modern science and technology, they have a better chance of surviving serious—even catastrophic—illnesses. That's the good news.

But, like every phonograph record, there's a flip side, and one with special significance for young adults. According to a report issued in 1979 by Dr. Julius Richmond, my predecessor as Surgeon General, Americans aged 15 to 24 had a higher death rate in 1979 than they did 20 years earlier. The causes: violent death and injury, alcohol and drug abuse, unwanted pregnancies, and sexually transmitted diseases. Adolescents are particularly vulnerable, because they are beginning to explore their own sexuality and perhaps to experiment with drugs. The need for educating young people is critical, and the price of neglect is high.

Yet even for the population as a whole, our health is still far from what it could be. Why? A 1974 Canadian government report attributed all death and disease to four broad elements: inadequacies in the health-care system, behavioral factors or unhealthy life-styles, environmental hazards, and human biological factors.

To be sure, there are diseases that are still beyond the control of even our advanced medical knowledge and techniques. And despite yearnings that are as old as the human race itself, there is no "fountain of youth" to ward off aging and death. Still, there is a solution to many of the problems that undermine sound health. In a word, that solution is prevention. Prevention, which includes health promotion and education, saves lives, improves the quality of life, and, in the long run, saves money.

In the United States, organized public health activities and preventive medicine have a long history. Important milestones include the improvement of sanitary procedures and the development of pasteurized milk in the late 19th century, and the introduction in the mid-20th century of effective vaccines against polio, measles, German measles, mumps, and other once-rampant diseases. Internationally, organized public health efforts began on a wide-scale basis with the International Sanitary Conference of 1851, to which 12 nations sent representatives. The World Health Organization, founded in 1948, continues these efforts under the aegis of the United Nations, with particular emphasis on combatting communicable diseases and the training of health-care workers.

But despite these accomplishments, much remains to be done in the field of prevention. For too long, we have had a medical care system that is science- and technology-based, focused, essentially, on illness and mortality. It is now patently obvious that both the social and the economic costs of such a system are becoming insupportable.

Implementing prevention—and its corollaries, health education and promotion—is the job of several groups of people:

First, the medical and scientific professions need to continue basic scientific research, and here we are making considerable progress. But increased concern with prevention will also have a decided impact on how primary-care doctors practice medicine. With a shift to health-based rather than morbidity-based medicine, the role of the "new physician" will include a healthy dose of patient education.

Second, practitioners of the social and behavioral sciences—psychologists, economists, city planners—along with lawyers, business leaders, and government officials—must solve the practical and ethical dilemmas confronting us: poverty, crime, civil rights, literacy, education, employment, housing, sanitation, environmental protection, health care delivery systems, and so forth. All of these issues affect public health.

Third is the public at large. We'll consider that very important group in a moment.

Fourth, and the linchpin in this effort, is the public health profession—doctors, epidemiologists, teachers—who must harness the professional expertise of the first two groups and the common sense and cooperation of the third, the public. They must define the problems statistically and qualitatively and then help us set priorities for finding the solutions.

To a very large extent, improving those statistics is the responsibility of every individual. So let's consider more specifically what the role of the individual should be and why health education is so important to that role. First, and most obviously, individuals can protect themselves from illness and injury and thus minimize their need for professional medical care. They can eat a nutritious diet, get adequate exercise, avoid tobacco, alcohol, and drugs, and take prudent steps to avoid accidents. The proverbial "apple a day keeps the doctor away" is not so far from the truth, after all.

Second, individuals should actively participate in their own medical care. They should schedule regular medical and dental checkups. Should they develop an illness or injury, they should know when to treat themselves and when to seek professional help. To gain the maximum benefit from any medical treatment that they do require, individuals must become partners in that treatment. For instance, they should understand the effects and side effects of medications. I counsel young physicians that there is no such thing as too much information when talking with patients. But the corollary is the patient must know enough about the nuts and bolts of the healing process to understand what the doctor is telling him. That is at least partially the patient's responsibility.

Education is equally necessary for us to understand the ethical and public policy issues in health care today. Sometimes individuals will encounter these issues in making decisions about their own treatment or that of family members. Other citizens may encounter them as jurors in medical malpractice cases. But we all become involved, indirectly, when we elect our public officials, from school board members to the president. Should surrogate parenting be legal? To what extent is drug testing desirable, legal, or necessary? Should there be public funding for family planning, hospitals, various types of medical research, and medical care for the indigent? How should we allocate scant technological resources, such as kidney dialysis and organ transplants? What is the proper role of government in protecting the rights of patients?

What are the broad goals of public health in the United States today? In 1980, the Public Health Service issued a report aptly entitled *Promoting Health-Preventing Disease: Objectives for the Nation.* This report expressed its goals in terms of mortality and in terms of intermediate goals in education and health improvement. It identified 15 major concerns: controlling high blood pressure; improving family planning; improving pregnancy care and infant health; increasing the rate of immunization; controlling sexually transmitted diseases; controlling the presence of toxic agents and radiation in the environment; improving occupational safety and health; preventing accidents; promoting water fluoridation and dental health; controlling infectious diseases; decreasing smoking; decreasing alcohol and drug abuse; improving nutrition; promoting physical fitness and exercise; and controlling stress and violent behavior.

For healthy adolescents and young adults (ages 15 to 24), the specific goal was a 20% reduction in deaths, with a special focus on motor vehicle injuries and alcohol and drug abuse. For adults (ages 25 to 64), the aim was 25% fewer deaths, with a concentration on heart attacks, strokes, and cancers.

Smoking is perhaps the best example of how individual behavior can have a direct impact on health. Today cigarette smoking is recognized as the most important single preventable cause of death in our society. It is responsible for more cancers and more cancer deaths than any other known agent; is a prime risk factor for heart and blood vessel disease, chronic bronchitis, and emphysema; and is a frequent cause of complications in pregnancies and of babies born prematurely, underweight, or with potentially fatal respiratory and cardiovascular problems.

Since the release of the Surgeon General's first report on smoking in 1964, the proportion of adult smokers has declined substantially, from 43% in 1965 to 30.5% in 1985. Since 1965, 37 million people have quit smoking. Although there is still much work to be done if we are to become a "smoke-free society," it is heartening to note that public health and public education efforts—such as warnings on cigarette packages and bans on broadcast advertising—have already had significant effects.

In 1835, Alexis de Tocqueville, a French visitor to America, wrote, "In America the passion for physical well-being is general." Today, as then, health and fitness are front-page items. But with the greater scientific and technological resources now available to us, we are in a far stronger position to make good health care available to everyone. And with the greater technological threats to us as we approach the 21st century, the need to do so is more urgent than ever before. Comprehensive information about basic biology, preventive medicine, medical and surgical treatments, and related ethical and public policy issues can help you arm yourself with the knowledge you need to be healthy throughout your life.

FOREWORD

Dale C. Garell, M.D.

Advances in our understanding of health and disease during the 20th century have been truly remarkable. Indeed, it could be argued that modern health care is one of the greatest accomplishments in all of human history. In the early 1900s, improvements in sanitation, water treatment, and sewage disposal reduced death rates and increased longevity. Previously untreatable illnesses can now be managed with antibiotics, immunizations, and modern surgical techniques. Discoveries in the fields of immunology, genetic diagnosis, and organ transplantation are revolutionizing the prevention and treatment of disease. Modern medicine is even making inroads against cancer and heart disease, two of the leading causes of death in the United States.

Although there is much to be proud of, medicine continues to face enormous challenges. Science has vanquished diseases such as smallpox and polio, but new killers, most notably AIDS, confront us. Moreover, we now victimize ourselves with what some have called "diseases of choice," or those brought on by drug and alcohol abuse, bad eating habits, and mismanagement of the stresses and strains of contemporary life. The very technology that is doing so much to prolong life has brought with it previously unimaginable ethical dilemmas related to issues of death and dying. The rising cost of health-care is a matter of central concern to us all. And violence in the form of automobile accidents, homicide, and suicide remain the major killers of young adults.

In the past, most people were content to leave health care and medical treatment in the hands of professionals. But since the 1960s, the consumer of medical care—that is, the patient—has assumed an increasingly central role in the management of his or her own health. There has also been a new emphasis placed on prevention: People are recognizing that their own actions can help prevent many of the conditions that have caused death and disease in the past. This accounts for the growing commitment to good nutrition and regular exercise, for the fact that more and more people are choosing not to smoke, and for a new moderation in people's drinking habits.

People want to know more about themselves and their own health. They are curious about their body: its anatomy, physiology, and biochemistry. They want to keep up with rapidly evolving medical technologies and procedures. They are willing to educate themselves about common disorders and diseases so that they can be full partners in their own health-care.

The ENCYCLOPEDIA OF HEALTH is designed to provide the basic knowledge that readers will need if they are to take significant responsibility for their own health. It is also meant to serve as a frame of reference for further study and exploration. The ENCYCLOPEDIA is divided into five subsections: The Healthy Body; The Life Cycle; Medical Disorders & Their Treatment; Psychological Disorders & Their Treatment; and Medical Issues. For each topic covered by the ENCYCLOPEDIA, we present the essential facts about the relevant biology; the symptoms, diagnosis, and treatment of common diseases and disorders; and ways in which you can prevent or reduce the severity of health problems when that is possible. The ENCYCLOPEDIA also projects what may lie ahead in the way of future treatment or prevention strategies.

The broad range of topics and issues covered in the ENCYCLOPEDIA reflects the fact that human health encompasses physical, psychological, social, environmental, and spiritual well-being. Just as the mind and the body are inextricably linked, so, too, is the individual an integral part of the wider world that comprises his or her family, society, and environment. To discuss health in its broadest aspect it is necessary to explore the many ways in which it is connected to such fields as law, social science, public policy, economics, and even religion. And so, the ENCYCLOPEDIA is meant to be a bridge between science, medical technology, the world at large, and you. I hope that it will inspire you to pursue in greater depth particular areas of interest, and that you will take advantage of the suggestions for further reading and the lists of resources and organizations that can provide additional information.

AUTHOR'S PREFACE

Air pollution is often a factor in the development of lung cancer.

At the beginning of the 20th century, a diagnosis of cancer was terrifying, a virtual death sentence—so much so that many doctors believed it was unethical to tell a patient his or her condition or even try to treat it. At that time, cancer was believed to be a nearly uncontrollable disease that struck randomly.

In fact, cancer has many forms, each with its own complicated origin. And the advent of computers, genetic engineering, and other weapons unknown just a few years ago has enabled molecular biologists and biochemists to study the many faces of the disease. Cancer remains a dangerous affliction, the second leading cause of death in the United States (heart disease is first), but the vast knowledge scientists are amassing concerning the nature of the disease has greatly improved both the quality and length of a cancer sufferer's life.

A BRIEF DEFINITION

Cancer is a general term used to indicate more than 100 separate diseases, all marked by the common characteristic of abnormal cell growth, or a breakdown in the body's growth-regulating mechanisms.

Sometimes called *malignant tumors*, or malignant neoplasms (neoplasm means "new growth"), cancers are classified according to the organs or tissues from which they originate. So, for instance, cancers that stem from cells that line the body's surfaces (internal or external) are called *carcinomas*. If they arise from bones and connective tissue, they are known as *sarcomas*; from blood or lymph systems, *leukemias* and *lymphomas*.

When the new growth or swollen mass emerges in one site and appears to be confined to it, doctors may call such an irregularity a "primary" cancer. If it enlarges and spreads nearby or to other organs and tissues, as is often the case, the cancer is called *metastatic* and the new colonies that have emerged, *metastases*.

THE ADVANTAGES OF EARLY DETECTION

When metastases do occur, they often do so in the liver, lymph nodes, bones, and brain. Some cancers spread quickly; others, hardly at all. It is now commonly believed that by the time some quick-spreading primary cancers are diagnosed, small clones of metastatic cells have entered nearby tissues or the bloodstream. Thus, many cancers that are detected early are treated locally with surgery and radiation to get at the primary site and body wide, or systemically, with drugs and other chemicals to try and "mop up" invisible colonies.

Because it is so essential to treat the cancer before it spreads, early detection is important to survival. According to *Cancer Facts and Figures—1989*, published by the American Cancer Society, patients who have lung cancer—one of the most deadly cancers—have a 5-year survival rate of 32% when the cancer is detected early and less than a 2% rate if the cancer is detected later and has spread. Ninety percent of women with breast cancer (which is very rare in men) who receive treatment while the cancer is localized are expected to reach the 5-year survival plateau, compared to 17% of patients whose cancer has spread by the time of diagnosis.

POSSIBLE FACTORS

In the 1970s, a new interest in ecology and the way it relates to health issues led many scientists to hypothesize that such environmental factors as air pollution, industrial chemical exposure, and water contamination were at least factors in the origin of most cancers. To this day, stories about a new cancer-causing chemical, food, or poison appear almost daily in the press. Most recently there have been reports that the gel-filled silicone used in breast implants causes cancer in some rats. Artificial sweeteners, hormones used in animal feed, and the invisible gas called radon that seeps from rock into homes have also stolen headlines.

Such stories are indeed true. Some toxic chemicals do alter cells and create cancers—at least in laboratory animals. But can-

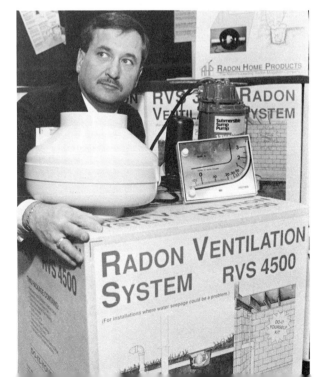

Radon gas is the leading cause of lung cancer, after cigarettes. It is a product of the natural decay of radium in the soil and is released from the foundations of and the ground beneath buildings.

cer is a complicated disease; there are many separate steps in the onset and progress of abnormal cell growth. Individual susceptibility to the disease plays a large role, and the results of tests performed on other animals can never completely replicate what happens in humans over a lifetime. Although scientists are identifying new cancer-causing substances at what seems to be an alarming rate, studies conducted by the National Institutes of Health and the American Cancer Society and published in the journal of the National Cancer Institute, as well as studies by independent investigators, suggest that "outside," or strictly environmental, triggers of cancer are not the chief villains.

Today, cancer-causing agents found in the workplace and in water and air probably account for fewer than 10% of all cancers, according to the American Cancer Society, although in the larger sense, most cancers are probably linked, or related, to physical surroundings, personal habits, or ways of life, including stressful living, unhealthy dietary habits, the use of tobacco and alcohol, and exposure to low-level radiation.

Stress, a bodily or mental reaction to demanding situations, disrupts the operations of both the endocrine and immune systems. Some believe this has an impact on the occurrence of cancer.

Get in touch with your body

Breast self-examination every month could save your life.

See your doctor, visit a health center or call your American Cancer Society for how to do it

The first defense against cancer is preventive education. In the late 1930s the New York City Cancer Committee directed its message to the public through posters mounted in subway cars.

This volume will discuss the nature of cancer: how it occurs, what its symptoms and consequences are, and what the miraculous methods of treatment are that, when employed early enough, can control it. Chapter 1 presents a brief history of the efforts scientists have made to identify and treat what was for many years a hopelessly fatal disease. Chapter 2 discusses the genetic and viral aspects of cancer, stressing that although the disease is not by nature a genetic disorder, every person possesses a small number of vulnerable genes whose activation is associated with malignant transformation of healthy cells. Chapter 3 outlines the contributing factors to cancer that can be controlled by the individual. Chapter 4 examines ways to test and detect cancerous tumors, stresses again how vital to survival early detection is, and offers some advice on the risk factors that teenagers and adults should be aware of. Chapter 5 explores the plight of children with cancer, emphasizing the tremendous progress medicine has made in combating a disease that once killed millions of children but can now be treated and often cured. The last three chapters of the book focus on cancer treatment: Chapter 6 discusses radiation, surgery, and chemotherapy; Chapter 7 explores future possibilities for even more effective treatment; and Chapter 8 concludes the volume with a look at cancer centers in the United States—their approaches to the disease and the progress they are making.

Cancer has always been a much-feared disease. Just a generation ago, many newspaper obituary columns would not mention the word *cancer*; they would list the cause of death of a cancer patient as a "lengthy illness." But public health education has removed much of the stigma that once accompanied a diagnosis of cancer and has replaced it with hopes for treatment and cure.

•   •   •   •

CHAPTER 1

· · · · · · · · · · · · · · · ·

A HISTORICAL
PERSPECTIVE

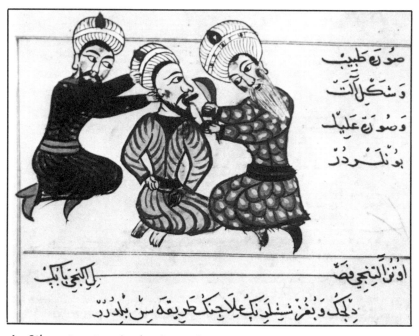

*An 8th-century treatise by the Arab conquerors of Spain—the Moors—
on the treatment of breast cancer.*

Doctors have been able to prevent, treat, and even cure some diseases without ever understanding how they develop. For example, in 1796 the English physician Edward Jenner was able to protect people from contracting deadly smallpox by deliberately infecting them with less virulent cowpox. This occurred long before anyone knew that smallpox was caused by a virus or knew how antibodies formed to fight disease. Jenner had simply observed that milkmaids who often caught cowpox rarely caught smallpox, and he used that observation to stop an epidemic.

Without any specific knowledge of the operation of viruses, Edward Jenner established the procedure of innoculation in 1796, when he discovered that he could prevent the development of smallpox by administering injections of cowpox.

This almost blind luck in discovering a cure has also been true for some forms of cancer. Surgeons were able to cure some patients of breast, colon, skin, and other malignancies long before much was known about the biology of these tumors. Ancient Greek physicians were able to surgically remove superficial tumors and even cancerous breasts. In the 11th century, Arab doctors practicing in Moorish Spain wrote texts on the surgical removal of cancers of the thigh and breast but warned that if the cancer was of "long standing and large, you should leave it alone."

Evidence that avoidance of cigarettes, alcohol, sunlight, and other "environmental" agents seemed to decrease the risk of some cancers was used by many physicians to prevent disease well before anyone really understood how cancer developed. The 18th-century British surgeon Sir Percival Pott, for instance, noted that chimney sweeps suffered a high rate of scrotal cancer because they were in constant contact with soot, even though the means by which such substances (now called hydro-carbons) caused cancer were unknown to him. He suggested correctly, however, that protective clothing could guard the men's health.

Over the next century, little substantial progress was made toward an understanding of the origin of cancer. As late as the 1890s, the New York surgeon Dr. William Bradford Coley was one of the few doctors who would even attempt to treat inoperable cancers. Coley had observed that the tumor of one of his cancer patients had grown smaller after the patient had contracted an almost fatal skin infection. So Coley injected a number of terminally ill cancer patients with bacterial poisons in an attempt to shrink their tumors. His experiment failed, but it demonstrates the almost desperate nature of cancer research at that time. But at least research had begun.

By the turn of the century it had become clear that only when they understood the behavior and biology of cancer could physicians hope to devise strategies to deal with the disease. A series of basic questions began to be addressed: In what cells do cancers

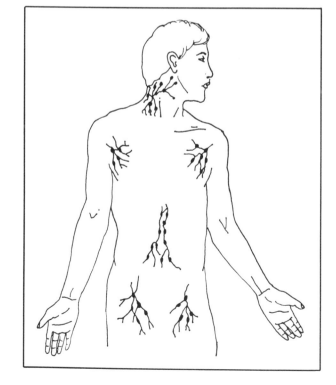

The nodes of the lymphatic system are located in the neck, abdomen, groin, and under the arms. When cancer invades the system, lymph nodes swell and lymphomas overrun the white blood cells.

arise? How do they spread? Why do some people seem more prone to cancer?

The questions came fast; the answers, slowly. Researchers who had studied smallpox, polio, or diphtheria had an easier job because all these diseases had a single, traceable cause: a virus or a bacterium. Once such tools as powerful microscopes were available, researchers could locate the germs that were responsible for a disease by inspecting tissues from patients, isolating the germs, and proving they caused the disease by injecting them into animals, culturing (growing) them, and observing their behavior. The germs then formed the basis of vaccines.

But when facing cancer, where should the researcher begin? First of all, there were dozens of variant forms of cancer with which to contend. Second, there existed few of the modern instruments that have recently opened up many new avenues of discovery. X rays for diagnosis and treatment were in their infancy and offered only crude views of internal structures. Scientists did not even know how to culture cancer cells in test tubes so that studies could be done with potentially curative drugs.

FINDING CLUES

It was only when the National Cancer Institute, the American Cancer Society, and other organizations began funding the major research efforts of the 1930s and 1940s that the first clues about cancer began to emerge. It was learned, for example, what cancer cells are: normal cells that have been altered in such a way that they manage not only to thwart the body's mechanisms that regulate and control normal cell development but also to elude the body's defense mechanisms. Unpredictable and canny, cancers grow and usurp other organs' supply lines of energy, colonize in hard-to-find places, and spread so invisibly that detection is often impossible.

In a brilliant series of experiments, Dr. Isaac Berenblum, an Israeli research pathologist and a professor emeritus of the Weizmann Institute in Rehovot, Israel, discovered what is now known as the two-stage model of cancer's origins. Dr. Berenblum exposed the skin of mice to a single dose of a hydrocarbon called *benzopyrene*, which causes normal cells to grow wildly. But he found that benzopyrene itself did not cause the malignancy. Next,

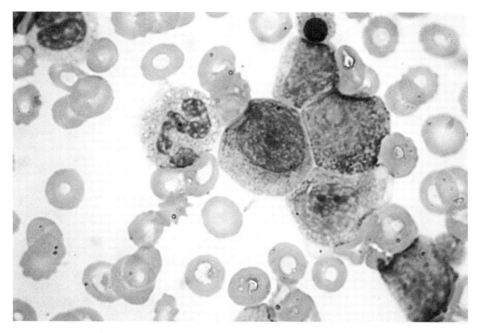

Cancer is classified into five different groups, depending on its location in the body; myelomas, pictured above, are tumors in the plasma cells of the bone marrow.

Berenblum irritated the mice's skin in a variety of ways, such as simple abrasion, and learned that irritation alone also did not cause cancer. He conducted similar experiments with a variety of other chemicals, including oil- and tar-based substances. He then tried chemicals and irritation in different orders—first irritant, then chemical, and vice versa, for example. Finally, he was able to conclude that some substances such as benzopyrene were able to initiate the cancerous process, whereas others were promoters, capable of speeding up and maintaining the process but unable to initiate it. And he concluded that both initiators and promoters were necessary to create the disease known as cancer.

What made this two-step model so useful in the understanding of cancer is that it seemed to confirm much of what scientists had observed about cancer in humans. It began to suggest how such environmental triggers as radiation and chemicals could interact with less obvious instigators of cancer. It helped explain why there could be such a long time interval between exposure to known cancer-causing agents and the development of cancer. And it introduced the very important notion—later confirmed in other experiments—that the origin and progress of the disease is not simple; that one "hit" by a causative substance is not sufficient to initiate the process and that the body's normal defense mechanisms probably dispose of numerous early-stage abnormal cells before they can metastasize.

If in fact cancer emerged in stages, doctors might enjoy an edge in detection, treatment, and prevention: Having identified exactly the various stages of each cancer as well as the initiators and promoters, they could intervene at any given stage in the process. Instead of a hopeless situation in which one hit could transform a normal cell forever into a cancerous cell, there would exist multiple opportunities to intercede in the process of malignancy.

Into the 1950s and 1960s, scientists working off of the two-stage model of cancer development sought and found an increasing number of initiators and promoters in both animals and man, including viruses and genes (see Chapter 2). They learned that some initiators damaged the whole cell, whereas others targeted the nucleus, where the genetic code resides. They learned that many organisms' vulnerability to initiation and promotion is related to the natural growth rate of the organisms themselves. These findings were critical to the development of successful *chemotherapy*, the use of drugs to attack cancer cells at their most vulnerable stages and cycles of growth.

Researchers have also found that some cancer cells resemble the early embryos of animals and that in some stages cancers behaved and grew very much like normal cells. As they pursued the biology of cancer, they found that cancer cells often contained proteins that are normally present only during periods of rapid prebirth growth in humans and other animals.

More Explanations

By the early 1970s scientists were at last able to offer a basic scenario of how cancer develops:

- Cells are exposed all the time to chemical, physical, viral, or genetic initiators, or stimulators, of cancer. Cancer arises, however, only when there is some kind of reaction between the initiators and a host cell that is already vulnerable or susceptible to stimulation.

Because some forms of cancer are not localized at a particular site, chemotherapies were developed that treat the whole system.

- Even after a cell is transformed into a cancer cell, the body's immune system can usually handle it unless there are many more successful cell divisions and much rapid growth. For some cancers, this can take weeks; for others, years.

- During this growth period, further exposure to promoters can influence whether the cancer survives or dies, but if it survives, it must at some stage develop its own blood supply for nourishment. To do this, cancers take the easiest route—wherever there is room to grow and the richest supply of blood vessels, they will flourish. Thus, soft tissues such as muscle, lymph nodes, and veins are often the first to be invaded by metastases. And that is why doctors can now prevent the cancer from spreading in many cases by using radiation or drugs on those areas even before the spreading cells are detectable.

- At various stages, many cancers can be destroyed by the body's immune system or by treatment of a small but detectable mass with surgery, radiation, or chemicals. But once the cancer has spread through the body, microscopic colonies may be undetectable and reachable only with intravenous chemicals, if at all.

The common characteristic of all cancers is that their cell population is composed of renegades that do not know when to stop dividing; they ignore the natural substances and instructions that regulate normal cell growth. The codes, or instructions, for controlling every cell's growth and other activities are contained in the cell's genes, located on chromosomes in the nucleus. Genes are composed of *DNA*, or deoxyribonucleic acid. Clearly, scientists were getting down to the essential facts of cancer. But they could not begin to study ways to treat and cure the disease until they took a careful look at the central control mechanism of cells—DNA.

• • • •

CHAPTER 2

GENES AND VIRUSES

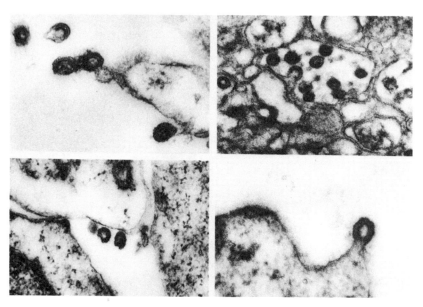

Recent research has located this leukemia virus—surrounded by a double membrane—in the cells of mice.

Scientists who have explored how a normal cell turns into a cancerous one have for a long time been struck by the way cancer seems to "run" in some families. Each year in the United States, for example, hundreds of couples are known to carry a 50% chance of bearing a child with a deadly form of eye cancer called *retinoblastoma*. In many families the sister and daughter of a breast-cancer sufferer have a rate of breast cancer many times the national average.

Such statistics provide strong support for the notion that whether or not a person gets cancer is decided at least in part by his or her inherited genetic codes. This notion has taken on even more meaning because the tools of genetic engineering have become widely available to probe the mechanisms of heredity.

Do some of a person's 50,000 to 100,000 genes, the strings of DNA that control cells and carry all hereditary information from parent to child, somehow play a role in the initiation of cancer? Could these genes be found? Can genes become damaged or altered in such a way as to make certain families more susceptible to cancer? Can the genes be eliminated, neutralized, or prevented from achieving expression? Are there genes that actually cause cancer directly? Can their presence be detected in an unborn child?

Today, the answer to all of these questions is yes, and the implications are exciting. The more scientists learn about the role of genes in cancer, the more opportunities there will be to intervene in the cancer process and to find ways to prevent and treat many more cases.

ONCOGENES

The prevalent modern view of cancer is that every person has a small number of genes in each of his or her cells that have the potential to transform normal cells into cancerous ones. These genes are known as *oncogenes* ("onco" from the Greek word *onkos*, meaning tumor or cancer). Moreover, studies show that all of these oncogenes arise initially from normal genes present in healthy cells.

In their normal form, these genes are called *proto-oncogenes*, and they control normal cell growth and development. But at some point their nature changes from commonplace to uncontrollably dangerous. Proto-oncogenes change into oncogenes when a virus, a chemical, radiation, or some accidental rearrangement of chromosomes that carry genes alters, or mutates, the genetic material of the cell.

GENES THAT DESTROY

It now seems certain that in every case of cancer, fragments of human DNA or genes are reprogrammed to destroy rather than carry on instructions for cell life. Cancer can be one result of that disruption. So far, scientists have found more than 40 animal and human oncogenes that play a role in cancer. Some estimate about 100 will have been found by this year.

The idea of oncogenes can be upsetting, because it creates the impression that everyone is walking around with little genetic time bombs just waiting to go off and cause cancer. But the good side of the story is, first, that the human body seems able to handle and suppress oncogenes with considerable efficiency. After all, most people do not get cancer. Second, the presence of cancer genes strongly suggests that cancer is not just a random piece of bad luck but a process that is subject to natural, biological laws, just as the universe is subject to physical laws. The presence of oncogenes means people have a good chance of understanding and being able to manipulate the rules by which cancer operates. What is already known about oncogenes also suggests that the vast majority of cancers are not inherited in the traditional sense of the word but are the result of a lifetime of harmful changes to genetic material after birth. That means that there may be decades of time in which to try to reduce the risk of activating oncogenes by avoiding radiation, chemicals, cigarettes, and any other materials that are known to activate them (see Chapter 4).

In short, cancer-gene research can show how normal cells guide their own growth, how cancer cells cannot, and how people can use that information to diagnose, prevent, and someday even cure cancer.

VIRUSES

The campaign to find and understand oncogenes began to emerge during the 1960s and 1970s, when scientists first began studying the nature of *viruses* that were known to cause cancer in animals. (Animal cancer viruses have never been shown to cause cancer in humans, although they can transform human cells in laboratory dishes and test tubes. No one can "catch" cancer from animals by being infected with animal tumor viruses.) Viruses are tiny pieces of "parasitic" DNA (a *parasite* is an organism that depends on another organism for support without contributing anything in return) with a thin protein coat on them. The animal tumor viruses that scientists have become especially interested

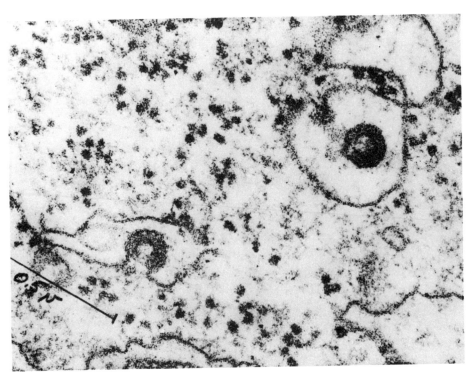

Electron micrograph of a leukemia cell, magnified 123,000 times, in liver of a guinea pig. The dark, round spot in upper right is a blood cancer virus being formed in a cell.

in are called *retroviruses*, which have the startling and unpleasant ability to invade a normal animal cell and reprogram the cell's normal genetic blueprint.

Experiments show that in each of these animal cancer viruses, a single piece of DNA or gene can make a cancer cell out of a healthy cell in chickens, rats, mice, birds, and monkeys. Studies have also demonstrated that these cancer genes are not, as their name suggests, virus genes at all, even though they are carried by viruses. Instead, they are nearly identical to normal genes. By comparing the phosphate building blocks of the normal and tumor-causing genes in a variety of organisms, from fruit flies to humans, scientists have concluded that perhaps half a billion years ago or more, certain viruses accidentally incorporated into their own genes copies of those of certain animals that they had infected. These "hitchhiker" genes sometimes included ones that caused cancer.

The full role viruses play in the cause of human cancer is uncertain, although at least four viruses are associated with human tumors. These are *hepatitis B* virus (which causes liver cancer), *papilloma virus* (associated with cervical and some other cancers), and the two human *T-lymphotropic* viruses, the best known of which—*HIV*—causes acquired immune deficiency syndrome, or AIDS. AIDS is marked by lowered immunity to life-threatening pneumonias and other infections and by a form of cancer called *Kaposi's sarcoma*.

These four viruses do not lead to cancer the way a polio virus, for example, leads to polio. They require cofactors, perhaps chemicals, irritants, radiation, or genetic changes, to lead to cancer.

The next part of the oncogeny story occurred when scientists realized how small a role animal retroviruses actually played in human cancer. There had to be some other link between genes and cancer, one that bypassed viruses. In 1982, researchers found it: genes in the DNA of human cancer cells that could transform normal cells grown in the laboratory into cancer cells. No viruses were involved. Scientists have since found that cells from many human cancers (lung, kidney, colon, blood, and breast) contain these genes.

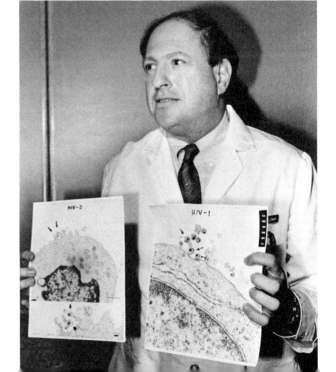

Dr. Lawrence Feldman of the University of Medicine in Newark, New Jersey, holds up microphotographs of HIV-1 and HIV-2 viruses that are one of the causes of Kaposi's sarcoma, a rare form of cancer.

CANCER GENES

Where do such human cancer genes come from if viruses do not carry them into the cells? The best research suggests that they arise from proto-oncogenes, the normal versions of cancer genes that have been conserved throughout evolution because they are needed to help regulate cell growth. When these precancerous genes are activated, or turned on in some abnormal way, they become cancer genes. There are at least three different ways that this can happen.

The first is for a tiny piece of DNA, a single pair of molecules in a single gene, to change, causing what is called a point mutation. Dr. Robert A. Weinberg, a molecular biologist at the Massachusetts Institute of Technology, discovered this change and described it in an article in *Nature* magazine in 1982. He compared a cancer gene in a bladder cancer cell to that gene's normal version in healthy tissue and found that the two shared everything but that one pair of molecules.

A second means by which cancer genes may be activated is by normal genes moving accidentally from one chromosome to another during the early stages of development, when growth occurs very rapidly. These accidental movements are called *chromosomal translocations*. One such translocation is known to cause *Burkitt's lymphoma*, a cancer of the lymph system. Scientists believe that the transfer of genes pulls a proto-oncogene away from neighbors that control it.

A third process that can activate cancer genes involves a dramatic amplification of oncogenes. For example, some colon cancer cells are known to have 30 to 50 times the number of an oncogene called *myo*. (All oncogenes are given three-letter names.) Multiple copies of genes have also been found in lung- and breast-cancer tissue. This multiplication probably occurs when an unusually large amount of protein (genes contain the code for making all proteins) encourages this uncontrollable cell growth.

Today, experts are looking more closely at the proteins that cancer genes produce because such proteins are likely to involve growth control. When these biochemical switches can be identified, isolated, and controlled, scientists will have powerful weapons for controlling both normal growth and cancer.

Beyond providing a new understanding of how cancer occurs, cancer genes are giving doctors new and better ways to diagnose and treat cancer. For example, scientists have discovered that some cancers are caused not by the presence of a bad gene but by the absence of a good, or protective, gene. Retinoblastoma, a rare eye cancer in children, is one such cancer. The absence or "deletion" of a protective gene in retinoblastoma is already being used to identify individuals who are susceptible to this disease. If a family is known to have a history of retinoblastoma, some genetic material can be sampled from an unborn child. If the antiretinoblastoma gene is not found, the risk to the child is easily established. Then efforts can be made to treat the cancer aggressively, as soon as the child is born, in order to save his or her life. Some couples have been reassured by the test that their unborn child is not at risk for retinoblastoma.

PROBING FOR ONCOGENES

Recent technological breakthroughs have enabled genetic engineers to probe human clusters of genes taken from blood and tissue samples to see if certain oncogenes are present and thus

Researchers have developed chemicals that can identify the presence of oncogenes.

to diagnose cancer in its early, most treatable stages. Using just such a DNA probe, scientists have found multiple copies of an oncogene called *neu* in some breast-cancer patients. These individuals have been found to have a much greater chance of suffering recurrences of their cancer than patients without the multiple copies, so they are cautioned to have more checkups and to be treated more aggressively.

A probe that could detect the difference between a protein made by a cancer gene and one in its normal state could be used to track the activation or lack of activation of cancer genes known to inhabit a person's cells. That would allow for extremely early diagnosis—and a better chance of cure—of leukemia and breast, lung, and colon cancers, all areas of intense research today.

As genetic-engineering methods advance, the time will come when scientists may be able to isolate cancer-resistant genes and overcome cancer-causing ones. Cancer gene probes may be used in conjunction with radiation or chemotherapy to search out and kill the cancer cells while leaving healthy cells alone. In this way, it may someday be possible to develop vaccines that boost the production of cancer-fighting proteins, or proteins that keep oncogenes or their switches turned to the "off" position.

•   •   •   •

CHAPTER 3

THE BASIC
STATISTICS

*Cigarettes are the primary cause of lung cancer,
which will strike 200,000 people in 1989.*

S tudying the biological nature of cancer is an important com-
ponent of understanding the disease. More frightening to
consider, however, is the threat cancer poses to each and every
person. This chapter reduces that threat to its essential numbers,
as reported by the American Cancer Society publication *Cancer
Facts and Figures—1989*. By their nature these are disturbing
statistics, but they also offer a powerful motive for altering one's
dietary and other habits to lessen the risk of cancer.

It is natural to feel "it can't happen to me," but the harsh reality
is that cancer can happen to anyone. The risk of cancer increases

with age, but cancer also kills more people between the ages of 3 and 14 than does any other disease. Of the some 250 million Americans now living, around 76 million will eventually get cancer—about 30%, according to present rates. In 1989 alone, about 1,010,000 Americans will be diagnosed as having cancer.

To understand these statistics properly, however, it is necessary to look at two important facts. First, there are many forms of cancer, and some forms are far more lethal than others. Second, there are many treatments for cancer. Surgery, radiation therapy, and chemotherapy are responsible for dramatically increasing the five-year survival rate for many kinds of cancer, and other techniques are in the works to combat cancer even more successfully. Taken together, these facts mean that one must look not just at the risk of getting cancer but at the risk of getting particular kinds of cancer.

It is simplest to categorize the forms of cancer according to the part of the body that the disease strikes. Categorized in this way, here are the basic statistics for selected cancer sites.

LUNG CANCER

In the United States there will be an estimated 155,000 new cases of lung cancer in 1989. Only 13% of patients diagnosed as having lung cancer will live 5 or more years after diagnosis, largely because lung cancer is very difficult to detect early. The main cause of lung cancer is smoking, however, and at the time of detected precancerous cellular changes, the damaged bronchial lining of the lungs often returns to normal—hence the critical need for smokers of all ages to undergo regular medical tests. The survival rate rises from 13% to 33% for cases in which the cancer is detected before it has spread to a large area of the lungs, but only 24% of lung cancers are detected that early.

BREAST CANCER

In the United States, there were an estimated 43,300 deaths (43,000 females, 300 males) from breast cancer in 1989. However, the large number of new cases of breast cancer treated in 1989—142,900—is attributed to the fact that many women now regularly undergo tests for signs of breast cancer and that early

Tobacco: Cash Crop and Killer

Americans have been smoking, chewing, and sniffing tobacco since 1612, when Virginia colonist John Rolfe started to cultivate tobacco plants. Skeptics suspected from the start that these practices could be unhealthy. But it was not until the early part of the 20th century that clinical findings established an unmistakably high correlation between the use of tobacco and various forms of illness, particularly cancer.

Antismoking movements arose even before the existence of scientific evidence linking smoking with cancer.

The most charismatic leader to appear in this movement was Lucy Gaston. In 1899 she founded the Chicago Anti-Cigarette League, a crusade that resulted in the opening of clinics to help cure smokers, and convinced several midwestern cities to ban the sale of tobacco. Whether or not she was directly responsible, cigarette sales dropped from 4.9 billion packs in 1897 to 3.5 billion in 1901.

The government added a chapter to the antismoking crusade in 1963, forming the Surgeon General's Advisory Committee on Smoking and Health. Although the committee was only a temporary panel of experts, two years later it became a permanent department, the National Clearinghouse for Smoking and Health (it was renamed the Office on Smoking and Health in 1978). One of the department's measures was to require cigarette manufacturers to print warnings on cigarette packs, announcing the hazards of smoking.

The establishment of the Surgeon General's committee highlighted a contradiction within the federal government's attempts to serve the public. Although the Surgeon General's Office decided it must protect the public's health, the Department of Agriculture continued to protect the financial well-being of tobacco farmers. Since the 1930s, the department has arranged to buy that portion of a tobacco farmer's crop that does not sell at the market rate— a rate established by the government—and to store the tobacco until prices improve. By 1986 the subsidy had risen to $155 million annually, a sum that attracted the wrath of health groups.

"The tobacco subsidy is untenable and abhorrent, and there's a lot of justification for ending it," said Dr. Ronald Davis, the American Medical Association's antismoking leader and a member of the AMA's board of trustees. "It is incongruous for the government to subsidize tobacco while warning that it causes cancer and heart disease."

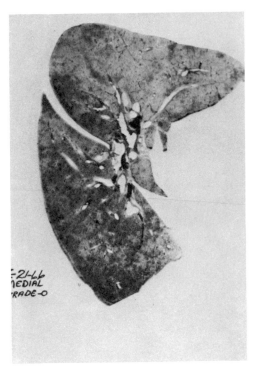
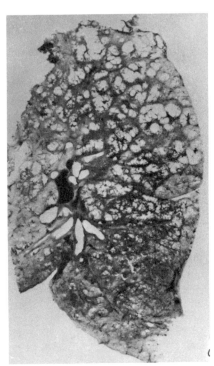

Left: *A healthy pair of lungs.* Right: *Lungs distended from years of inhaling cigarette smoke.*

detection greatly increases the chances of successful treatment. The 5-year survival rate for localized breast cancer is now 90%; if the cancer has spread, however, the survival rate is 60%. The lesson of these figures is that regular medical checkups are essential. The American Cancer Society recommends a professional physical examination of the breast every 3 years for women between the ages of 20 and 40 and every year for women over 40. Although most breast lumps are not cancer, only a physician can tell, and anyone with a breast lump should have a checkup immediately.

COLON AND RECTUM CANCER

In the United States there will be an estimated 53,500 deaths from colon cancer and 7,800 deaths from rectum cancer in 1989. Combined, these two forms of cancer are second in mortality only to lung cancer. There will be about 151,000 new cases in 1989: 107,000 of colon cancer and 44,000 of rectum cancer. When these forms of cancer are discovered at an early, localized stage, the 5-year survival rate is 87% for colon cancer and 79% for rectum cancer. If the cancer has spread, however, the survival rates fall to 40% and 31%, respectively. The American Cancer Society recommends an annual rectal examination every year after the age of 40. Every person over the age of 50 should have a blood stool slide test every year, and a *proctosigmoidoscopy*, or "procto" exam, every 3 to 5 years. As with other forms of cancer, early detection of colon and rectum cancer can greatly increase one's chances of survival.

UTERINE CANCER

In the United States there will be an estimated 10,000 deaths in 1989 from the 2 forms of uterine cancer: 6,000 deaths from cervical cancer and 4,000 from endometrial cancer. Due to the *Pap*

A mammogram, or soft-tissue X ray of the breast, is an important tool in the detection of breast cancer.

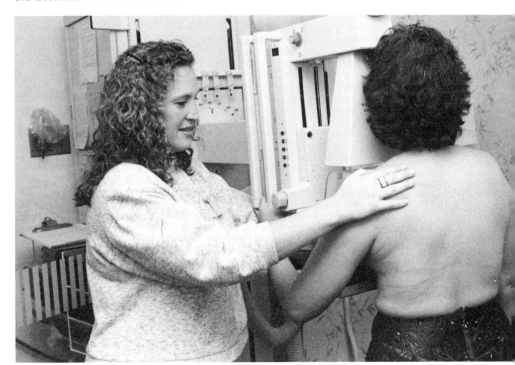

test and regular checkups, the mortality rate for uterine cancer has fallen more than 70% during the last 40 years. There will, however, be an estimated 52,000 new cases in 1989: 13,000 of cervical cancer and 39,000 of endometrial cancer. The 5-year survival rate for cervical cancer diagnosed early is 80% to 90%. Endometrial cancer afflicts mostly mature women, detected most frequently when they are between the ages of 55 and 69. Cervical cancer can afflict women of all ages, but young women who have intercourse at an early age and with different partners may be more susceptible, presumably because they are exposed to more sexually transmitted diseases. Women who are or have been sexually active or who are 18 years of age or older should have an annual Pap test and pelvic exam to check for cervical cancer. The Pap test is highly effective for detecting cervical cancer but only 50% effective for detecting endometrial cancer. Women at high risk of developing endometrial cancer (that is, women with a history of failure of ovulation, infertility, or prolonged estrogen therapy and obesity) should have an endometrial tissue test performed at the time of menopause.

OVARIAN CANCER

There will be an estimated 12,000 deaths from ovarian cancer in 1989. Ovarian cancer causes more deaths than any other cancer of the female reproductive system. There will be about 20,000 new cases of ovarian cancer diagnosed in 1989. The risk of developing this form of cancer increases with age—the highest rates are for women between the ages of 65 and 84. The American Cancer Society recommends that women over the age of 40 have a pelvic examination every year. If ovarian cancer is detected early, the 5-year survival rate is about 85%; diagnosis at a more advanced stage reduces the survival rate to 23%. The survival rate for all patients is 38%.

SKIN CANCER

There will be an estimated 8,200 deaths caused by skin cancer in the United States in 1989. Six thousand of these will result from malignant melanoma; the other 2,200 will be due to a variety of other skin cancers. However, there will be an estimated 500,000 cases of skin cancer diagnosed in the United States in 1989; 27,000 of these will be malignant melanoma, the most serious form of skin cancer. The number of cases of malignant melanoma is increasing by 3.4% a year. One of the chief dangers of malignant melanoma is that it can quickly spread to other parts of the body; however, with early detection it is highly curable, as are the other less serious forms of skin cancer such as basal-cell and squamous-cell cancers. The 5-year survival rate for patients with *malignant melanoma* that is detected early is 80%. The survival rate for other kinds of skin cancer is 95%.

LEUKEMIA

About 18,000 people in the United States will die of leukemia in 1989. Of the 27,300 people who will be diagnosed as having the disease, some 25,000 will be adults, and 2,300 will be children. The most common form of leukemia for children is acute lymphocytic leukemia, which will strike an estimated 1,800 children in 1989. For adults, the most common forms are acute granulocytic leukemia (approximately 8,000 cases in 1989) and chronic lymphocytic leukemia (approximately 9,600 cases annually).

Overall, the 5-year survival rate for white patients is 33%; for black patients it is 28%. These figures, however, are due in part to the poor survival rate of those with a few types of leukemia, such as acute granulocytic.

The forms of cancer listed above represent only some of the major types; others include prostate cancer (with 28,500 deaths per year), oral cancer (an estimated 8,650 deaths in 1989), bladder cancer (an estimated 10,200 deaths in 1989), and pancreatic cancer (an estimated 25,000 deaths in 1989). Overall, some 502,000 Americans will die of some form of cancer in 1989— 1,375 people a day, or one person every 63 seconds. Moreover, the death toll is rising: In 1930 the number of cancer deaths in the United States per 1,000 people was 143; in 1940 it was 152; by 1986 it was 171.

This overall increase is largely due to the dramatic rise in one particular form of cancer—lung cancer. The death rates for most other forms of cancer have leveled off over the last 50 years and in some cases have fallen. It is heartening that so many forms of cancer are not increasing, but these statistics point out something equally important: that a remarkably high number of cancer deaths are in a sense self-inflicted, by people who choose to smoke, choose not to stop, and opt not to follow a sensible diet.

• • • •

CHAPTER 4

REDUCING THE
RISKS OF
CANCER

Foods with a high fat content are sometimes factors in the development of cancer.

Taking risks is a part of everyday life. Some risks might seem worth taking, such as asking for a raise. Other risks are foolish: Failing to wear a seat belt while in a car can result in life in a wheelchair, and smoking crack even once may mean death. The risks most young people take usually have immediate consequences. Understandably, young people are concerned with the present and less with the distant future. Old age seems (and is) a lifetime away and therefore young people do not think much about risks that may influence their health decades from now.

But the risks involving cancer are measured not in hours, days, or weeks but over years and generations. Cancer can take 10, 20, 30, or 40 years to emerge. Cancer also involves many cofactors, both internal and external, interacting over long periods of time. It is therefore difficult to determine whether avoiding a particular behavior is definitely going to reduce the risk of a bad consequence the way wearing a seat belt will reduce the risk of a fatal or crippling auto accident.

No one suggests that teenagers ought to worry daily about the risk of getting cancer, heart disease, or any other disorder. Nor is it implied that they should live a Spartan life of self-denial that eliminates every hamburger, every day at the beach, or every habit that might somehow increase their risk of getting sick someday. But because of the cumulative nature of cancer development, many scientists do suggest that some actions that reduce the risk of cancer are so critical that they are worth starting at a young age.

"We know now that to some degree cancer can be a preventable disease," according to Dr. Vincent T. DeVita, Jr., for 10 years the director of the National Cancer Institute. "One third of cancers result from smoking cigarettes (cancers of the lung, bronchial and esophagus, for example). . . . Thirty-five percent of cancers (ones of the digestive tract, colo-rectal and stomach) are related to diet. Studies conducted during the war years in England show a true decline in cancer during the three or four years when people were forced by circumstances to follow a restricted diet, high in vegetables and low in animal fats. If you eat a sensible diet, you reduce your risk of cancer and of other diseases as well. So because between one third of cancers are due to smoking and another 35 percent are related to diet, we can reduce cancer incidence significantly," he concludes, by just paying attention to those two factors.

Unmistakable Facts

There are, of course, people who say that there is no absolute "proof" that quitting smoking or altering one's diet will reduce the risk of cancer. What these people do not understand, however, or choose to ignore, is the difference between reducing risk and guaranteeing prevention. It is hard to ignore the mountain of evidence concerning risk factors and cancer—facts such as the following:

- A study by Sir Richard Doll of Oxford University compared the incidence of cancer (the percentage of people who get cancer) among British doctors who smoked and British doctors who did not. It concluded that lung-cancer deaths were 31 times more frequent among smokers than among nonsmokers and that many more cancers of the mouth and lips, which most commonly are benign tumors and wartlike growths or tumors of the blood vessels, were recorded in smokers than in nonsmokers.

- A similar study by E. Cuyler Hammond and Daniel Horn of the American Cancer Society monitored cancer deaths in a group of 187,783 Americans for more than 3 years and found almost the same differences in lung-cancer rates as did Professor Doll.

- By the 1980s, more than a thousand studies had confirmed that 85% of all lung-cancer cases are directly connected to smoking. And the 1982 Surgeon General's Report, *The Health Consequences of Smoking: Cancer*, concludes that up to 40% of bladder cancers, 30% of pancreatic cancers, and a large percentage of cancers of the larynx and mouth are also due to smoking.

- More than a hundred articles have confirmed that passive smoking (inhaling the smoke of another's pipe, cigarette, or cigar) increases one's risk of getting cancer. One typical study, published in 1986 in the British journal *The Lancet*, compared 369 cancer patients with the same number of cancer-free subjects, all similar in age, smoking habits, and ways of life. The study found that the more smokers with whom a person shared living space, the greater the risk of cancer of the lung, pharynx, esophagus, pancreas, urinary tract, cervix, breast, and blood.

- Snuff and chewing tobacco users are 13 times more likely to suffer cheek and gum cancers than nonusers, according to a study published by the National Cancer Institute and the University of North Carolina and published in the *New England Journal of Medicine* in 1981.

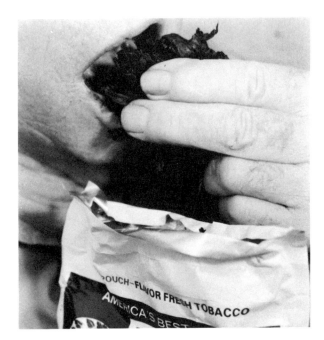

Cigarettes are not the only form of tobacco to cause cancer. Users of chewing tobacco and snuff are 13 times more likely to get cancer than nonusers.

- In a study of more than a million Americans over age 30, the American Cancer Society collected 300 separate pieces of information on everything from occupation and marital status to bowel habits. These people were studied for more than 13 years. The results definitively pinned down the direct relationship between smoking and cancer. A similar study by the society has begun to draw some tough links between dietary fat, cholesterol, alcoholism and a variety of cancers.

- By experimenting with the diets of animals, scientists can manipulate the incidence of cancer by adding or taking away such nutrients as vitamin A, antioxidants used as food preservatives, alcohol, fats, vitamin C, fiber, beta-carotene (a chemical found in carrots), and mustards and cabbage-family foods called crucifers.

- By studying the patterns of diseases in entire countries and even continents, epidemiologists have learned that sunlight can be responsible for melanomas and basal-cell and squamous-cell carcinomas; that salt and other preservatives can cause stomach and esophageal cancer;

that the age at a first pregnancy can determine the onset of breast cancer; and that obesity can bring about cancer of the uterus, colon, and gall bladder.

SOME CASE STUDIES

An early example of an attempt to identify the factors that cause cancer dates from 1700, when the Italian physician Bernardio Ramazzini noticed that nuns seemed to have a high susceptibility to breast cancer. There were many differences in the way nuns lived compared to other women, and celibacy was the major one. Ramazzini concluded that celibacy is a risk factor for breast cancer. It took centuries for him to be proved partially correct—hormones secreted during pregnancy exert protective effects for some women against breast cancer. To be sure, noncelibate women who do not get pregnant are as susceptible to breast cancer as are celibate women. Although slightly flawed, Ramazzini's observations helped establish the link between living habits and cancer.

Few case studies concerning diet and cancer are as dramatic as that of the Japanese and stomach cancer. Japanese people who are born and live out their life in Japan have a higher-than-average rate of cancer; Japanese people who move at an early age to the United States have a much lower rate than do their compatriots who remain at home. Japanese children who are born and live their entire life in the United States have even lower rates. Clearly, where a person lives and the diets and other habits open to him make a difference. That information has been used to help Japanese people living in Japan alter their native diets and reduce the risk of stomach cancer.

Another interesting link between national dietary habits and cancer occurs in India. Thirty percent of all cancer victims in that country suffer from mouth cancer, as a result of the Indian habit of eating a paste containing lime, betel nut, and tobacco flakes that constantly irritates the tender membranes of the mouth. In one part of South Africa, Bantu men have an exceptionally high rate of esophageal cancer, and scientists believe it is due to their drinking a locally brewed beer that contains a known cancer-causing agent called nitrosamine. And the way some of Iran's nomadic peoples make their bread—in open earth ovens that contaminate the bread with soot—almost certainly explains why they also have a high rate of esophageal cancer.

REDUCING RISKS

The National Cancer Institute believes so strongly in the ability to apply what is already known about risk factors to reduce cancer risk that it has set an astonishing goal: It plans to reduce the U.S. cancer death rate by 50% by the year 2000. Its experts believe it can be done by continuing to identify habits, substances, and other risks that are strongly linked to cancer and by finding new ways to detect cancers earlier, when they are most curable. These same experts are even more excited by the prospect of reducing cancer deaths if they can persuade teenagers to begin reducing risks now.

The first step for teenagers is to understand which cancers are the most likely to strike them as they age. For example, if a 13 year old lives in Alaska, where amounts of sun exposure are very limited, the likelihood of getting sunburn-related melanoma and other skin cancer is far less then if he or she lives in the American Southeast. If a 17 year old lives or works around such chemicals as asbestos, nickel, vinyl chloride, or chromate, the risk of certain cancers of the lung and digestive organs is higher than usual, especially if he or she smokes as well.

Exposure to sunlight has been proven to cause melanomas and squamous-cell and basal-cell carcinomas.

Along with this general awareness, every person should have regular tests and checkups to detect cancers that might arise at the earliest, most curable stages. All women 18 years of age or older should have a Pap smear every year to test for cervical cancer. A Pap smear involves taking a small sample of tissue from the woman's cervix and examining it for irregular cells.

The American Cancer Society also recommends monthly breast self-examination by all women 20 or older, manual exams given by a doctor, and a mammogram test every year for women who are at especially high risk at any age. (High-risk women are those with a family history of breast cancer, a history of cancer elsewhere in the body, "lumpy" breasts that are hard to self-examine, and hormonal imbalances.)

Dentists should check their patients' mouth, especially the mouths of smokers, at least annually for suspicious irritations. Many teenagers and young adults have chronic bowel problems, usually constipation. Each year, some 151,000 people develop cancer of the colon or rectum, and 53,000 die of the disease. These cancers can be diagnosed early with rectal and bowel examinations. More than 90% of all people with bowel cancer have microscopic traces of blood in their stool. Therefore, those who have a family history of colon or rectum cancer or have bleeding from the rectum or a history of constipation or bowel pain should have a rectal and bowel examination each year or whenever symptoms are chronic. There are also simple home tests, called Hemoccult tests, that can be used to detect blood in the stool. A stool sample is placed on a special surface and sealed, then mailed or taken to a lab for study. That "occult" blood is found does not indicate cancer, only a suspicion of it and the need for a proctosigmoidoscopic examination, in which a lighted flexible tube is used to examine the lining of the bowel.

Beginning at about age 20, everyone should have a cancer-related checkup approximately every 3 years. Any of the so-called seven early warnings of cancer demand a checkup right away. These signs are as follows:

1. A change in bowel or bladder habits.

2. A sore that does not heal anywhere on the skin or elsewhere.

3. Unusual bleeding or discharge.

4. A thickening or lump in the breast or elsewhere.

5. Indigestion or difficulty in swallowing.

6. An obvious change in a wart or mole.

7. A nagging cough or hoarseness.

The six cancer sites that offer the greatest targets for prevention or early cure are the colon, rectum, lung, breast, uterus, mouth, and skin, which collectively account for about half of all cancer deaths in older age groups.

In the United States, the most frequent cancers, in descending order for men, are of the lung, prostate, colon and rectum, urinary tract, and blood and blood-forming tissues. For women, they are cancers of the breast, colon and rectum, lung, uterus and cervix, and blood and blood-forming tissues.

FAMILY HISTORY

Knowledge of family history of cancer is important, too. If an individual's parents or close relatives have, or have died from, cancers of the breast, colon, rectum, leukemia, or any of the inherited cancers (see Chapter 2), his or her risk may be greater than usual, and he or she may need to have more frequent checkups and pay more attention to certain risk factors known to be associated with those cancers.

For example, a teenage girl whose mother and maternal grandmother both have breast cancer has a breast-cancer risk many times greater than a girl without such a family history. This is especially true if her mother had breast cancer before the age of 40.

This does not mean she is doomed to get breast cancer, only that her risk is higher. She may want to learn breast self-examination and have special X rays called mammograms earlier in her life and more frequently than someone without such a family history. Such measures will greatly reduce her risk.

The next step in reducing risk is to understand which risk factors are associated with which cancers. Exposure to tobacco, for instance, is linked to cancers of the lung, larynx, throat, esophagus, pancreas, bladder, brain, and lymphs. Exposure to alcohol

As this sign indicates, inhaling smoke from someone else's cigarette can be almost as dangerous as smoking itself. In 1988 New York City passed a law restricting smoking to designated areas.

is linked to cancers of the liver, brain, lymphs, and esophagus. A family history of cancer in the ovary, colon, uterus, breast, and skin increases the risk of those cancers but not others. Certain infections, such as hepatitis B and AIDS, often lead to cancer of the liver and leukemia. And colon polyps—benign growths in the intestine—put many people at a higher than usual risk of colon cancer.

Here are some steps that experts at the American Cancer Society, National Cancer Institute, and other public health institutions believe are worth taking immediately to reduce the risk of contracting cancer:

- Stop the use of all forms of tobacco. "There is no single action an individual can take to reduce the risk of cancer more effectively than to quit smoking," says Surgeon General C. Everett Koop of the U.S. Public Health Service. Better yet, never start smoking. Tobacco is highly addictive, and once started, the smoking habit is hard to break.

- Limit the amount of time spent in the sun and avoid by all means a blistering sunburn. Overexposure to sunlight is the major cause of almost every one of the 500,000 cases of nonfatal skin cancer each year. But recent studies show that accumulated exposure to the sun over many years is also a major contributor to melanoma, a more dangerous form of skin cancer that can spread to other parts of the body. Anyone who enjoys sitting in the sun should use effective sunblock agents, wear protective clothing, and stay out of the sun if possible during mid- and late afternoon hours, when the sun is most intense. Tanning parlors should also be used with caution; they are as dangerous as direct sunlight.

- Use alcohol moderately, if at all. The more people drink, the higher their risk of mouth, throat, liver, bladder, and other cancers.

- Keep exposure to radiation—even medical X rays—to the minimum allowable for good health. Although radiation is a tremendously important tool in the diagnosis and treatment of many cancers, it is also a potent destroyer of DNA and therefore—ironically—can itself cause cancer. Marie Curie and her husband, Pierre, the discoverers of radium, both died of cancer, as did their daughter and son-in-law, who worked with them unaware of the risks. In the 1950s, some doctors treated infections of the tonsils and thymus gland, and some skin rashes, with large doses of X rays, making their patients susceptible decades later to cancers of these organs.

The American Cancer Society and other groups recommend that chest X rays, dental X rays, and other diagnostic X rays never be performed without good medical indication and always in hospitals or doctors' offices where the X-ray equipment is licensed, certified, and modern so as to assure the least radiation exposure with each film. The American Cancer Society stopped recommending annual chest X rays in 1980, even to detect lung cancer in adults who are heavy smokers. Studies suggest, the American Cancer Society says, that up to a third of X rays provide no useful or new information to doctors.

One of the reasons there has been so much controversy over annual breast X rays for women under 45 is that there is fear that such regular exposure to radiation might in itself increase the risk of cancer and outweigh the benefit of the mammogram in detecting early, curable tumors. Now, however, the American Cancer Society and National Cancer Institute both recommend annual mammograms for women 40 and over and at least a baseline (defining test) at age 35. This is in large part because of evidence that the benefits outweigh the risks and because of newer equipment that reduces the amount of radiation needed to produce good X-ray images.

- One should check with the public health department about possible risk of radon exposure in one's home. Radon is a colorless, odorless gas that can, over long periods in high enough concentrations, increase the risk of cancer. Detectors are available to identify radon sources, and homes with radon can be made safe.

- Be aware of occupational carcinogens. Those who work in a gasoline station should wear protective gloves, boots, and pants to limit exposure to petrochemicals on their skin. Factory workers should know which chemicals they come in contact with, wear recommended

Exposure to hazardous chemicals at the workplace can trigger the development of cancer.

safety gear, and report safety violations to authorities. Carpenters are at risk of nasal cancer from wood dust; miners are more prone to cancers of the lung, bone, liver, and skin from coal, iron oxide, and uranium; shoe-makers show a higher than normal rate of leukemia from exposure to benzene; and welders are more prone to cancers of the kidney, lung, and prostate from exposure to cadmium.

- Be aware that exposure to toxic fumes, gases, vapors, dust, certain dyes, formaldehyde, and arsenic increases cancer risk. And many toxic chemicals are found in art and hobby supplies, paints, and household cleaning items. For example, people who have hobbies associated with metal may make use of iron oxides, nickels, and benzenes. All of these compounds are carcinogenic. However, they can all be safely used if the proper precautions are taken: gloves, masks, adequate ventilation to dissipate fumes, and regular checkups of the skin and lungs.

- One's diet should be low in fat and high in fiber. Obese people have a higher risk of developing colon, breast, and uterine cancers, and high-fat diets may be a major reason why. Changing one's diet to reduce the risk of cancer is sometimes called *chemoprevention*.

High-fiber foods and diets are believed to prevent cancer by speeding up the passage of potentially cancer-causing waste products through the intestinal tract. The idea behind fiber as a cancer-risk reducer emerged in studies of various groups of people in primitive and developed societies who had low- and high-fiber diets and telling rates of colon and rectum cancer. Cultures and tribes that ate a lot of roughage and fiber (often because more expensive kinds of foods, such as refined and processed items and protein, were not available) had a much lower incidence of bowel cancer. And people who ate a low-fiber, high-fat, high-protein diet had a correspondingly higher incidence of these diseases.

High-fiber foods—bran cereals, salad foods, and cruciferous vegetables such as broccoli and cauliflower—are also a healthy replacement for high-fat foods, which can also pose a risk to the

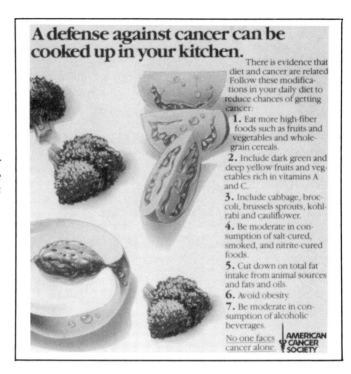

A defense against cancer can be cooked up in your kitchen. There is evidence that diet and cancer are related. Follow these modifications in your daily diet to reduce chances of getting cancer:

1. Eat more high-fiber foods such as fruits and vegetables and whole-grain cereals.

2. Include dark green and deep yellow fruits and vegetables rich in vitamins A and C.

3. Include cabbage, broccoli, brussels sprouts, kohlrabi and cauliflower.

4. Be moderate in consumption of salt-cured, smoked, and nitrite-cured foods.

5. Cut down on total fat intake from animal sources and fats and oils.

6. Avoid obesity.

7. Be moderate in consumption of alcoholic beverages.

No one faces cancer alone. AMERICAN CANCER SOCIETY

The American Cancer Society issued these dietary guidelines in 1986.

heart. Foods rich in vitamins A and C may lower the risk of cancers of the larynx, esophagus, stomach, and lungs.

- Avoid salt-cured, smoked, and deli foods cured with nitrates, which are used to preserve and add color to lunch meats. By themselves most preservatives are not carcinogens, but nitrates, for example, are readily converted to nitrites in the stomach and may in that form help produce nitrosamines, which are very carcinogenic.

There are many other chemicals that have produced cancer in test animals, but one must use common sense in deciding whether to avoid them altogether. "No human diet can be entirely free of mutagens or agents that can be carcinogenic in rodents," says Dr. Bruce Ames, a biochemist at the University of California at Berkeley and an expert on experimental cancer research. "We need to identify the important causes of human cancer among the vast number of minimal risks." The important causes are the ones to worry about first.

Dr. Ames's advice could be applied equally to the whole spectrum of cancer risks. Simple common sense tells one that when confronted with something as potentially lethal as cancer, the only reasonable course of action is to eliminate the main risks first. By doing this—by avoiding smoking, overexposure to the sun, excessive use of alcohol, exposure to radiation, and known carcinogenic substances in one's diet—one can dramatically reduce his or her chances of developing cancer.

•   •   •   •

CHAPTER 5

TREATING AND CURING CANCER: THE BIG THREE

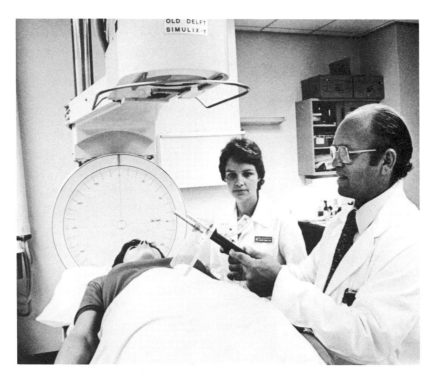

Radiation therapy.

Many doctors are still reluctant to use the word *cure* when they talk to cancer patients and their families about treatment. Since the 1970s, however, cancer treatments have improved so dramatically that more than a dozen types of cancer are considered curable. And victims of dozens of other types of cancer are guaranteed to live long and productive lives if they receive proper medical care. "I can foresee the day," writes Dr. Vincent T. DeVita, Jr., "when cancer is no worse than a chronic

In the 4th century B.C. Hippocrates, the ancient Greek physician, described the removal of cancerous tissue from breasts.

disease. The most surprising thing about cancer today is that half [of all cases] . . . are curable."

The increase in the cure rate from nearly zero in 1900 to 50% in 1989 is largely due to the 3 mainstays of cancer treatment: surgery, radiation, and chemotherapy. Often these approaches are used in various combinations, depending on the strength of the cancer and whether it has spread to a secondary site. The expertise of several physicians is usually enlisted in patient care, and they are assisted by teams of technicians, nurses, and pharmacologists. At their disposal are dozens of anticancer drugs, antibiotics—erythromycin, penicillin, and the cephalosporins that counteract the germs—that are used to prevent or treat post-operative infections, special protein-rich diets, and medicines—especially antiemetics such as Phenergan that treat nausea and vomiting—to combat the side effects of radiation and chemotherapy. In medical centers and regional cancer hospitals, all of this expertise converges in one place as medical experts approach the treatment of each case of cancer as a major contest, with game plans and strategists and backup positions.

SURGERY

Surgery is the primary form of therapy. It is used by itself when the doctor can be reasonably sure that none of the cells from the diseased tissue will spread from the site into the lymph system, which would allow it to spread throughout the body. The Greek physician Hippocrates described removal of breasts that were diseased with cancer in the 4th century B.C. But what is known today as surgical oncology could not really get under way until anesthesia and antiseptic techniques controlled the pain and injury of surgery. By the end of the 19th century, Dr. Theodor Billroth of Vienna used both techniques to remove stomach cancers.

Today, surgery is performed not only with scalpels but also with *lasers*, which are highly concentrated sources of heat and power held in a highly focused beam of amplified light waves that cut through tissue with a precision that leaves surrounding tissues undamaged. Surgeons also use electric cautery (a process of searing or burning by the application of an electric charge), chemical solvents, and deep cold to destroy unwanted tissue on the surface or in areas of the body such as the face, where precision cutting means less cosmetic damage. Plastic and reconstructive surgery are used to restore both form and function to skin and other organs altered by cancer therapy. Surgery has thus become a highly refined technique for cancer treatment, but the use of X rays and chemotherapy as partners in cancer care is making drastic surgery a much less common, and less necessary, procedure.

Radical mastectomy, for example, a surgical treatment for breast cancer that once involved the removal not only of a woman's cancerous breast but also of much of the chest wall behind it to arrest any spreading of cells to that area, has today been modified to preserve the chest wall and muscle. The same or even a higher cure rate is possible with today's mastectomy procedures because drugs and X rays can now be used to eliminate cancer cells that surgery may have missed and because doctors now have better methods to detect and attack any cancer recurrences. Dr. Gianni Bonnadonna of the Cancer Institute of Milan, Italy, found that after 5 years, 69.4% of women treated with mastectomies and drugs together were still alive, compared to only 44.3% of those treated with surgery alone. And in Finland, a study of 702 women has suggested that, at least for women under 65, a lumpectomy, or simple removal of a cancerous lump in the breast followed by radiation, may prove more effective in saving lives than full removal of the breast itself.

Cancer surgery takes several forms. Sometimes it is used to prevent cancer, as when intestinal polyps or skin moles that are known to have a high risk of becoming cancerous are removed before they become malignant. Surgery is used to detect cancer as well; through an operation called a *biopsy*, a small sample of body tissue is removed and examined to see if it is in fact cancerous. Surgery is also used to "stage" the disease (to find out how far it has spread) and to remove all known evidence of a particular cancer.

With some forms of cancer, surgery is performed to control symptoms, reduce pain, and in general improve the quality of life even when cure is not possible. This is called *palliative surgery*. It works by reducing the "tumor burden" that the body must bear. Some cancers are so large that they exhaust the body's ability to nourish them, or they press against vital nerves, bones, and other organs, creating pain and even paralysis. In these instances, surgical reduction of the tumor makes the patient feel better even if cure is not possible. And when patients feel better, they eat better, move better, and sleep better.

RADIATION

After Wilhelm Conrad Röntgen discovered X rays in 1895 and, three years later, Marie and Pierre Curie discovered radium rays, scientists were intrigued by the ability of these rays to pass through solid objects and to leave a permanent record (on a light-sensitive plate, for example) of the relative density of the object through which they had passed. This meant that for the first time doctors could examine, without surgery, the bones and muscles of the human body.

Less positive effects of radiation included pain, burns, sores, and other damaging effects to humans exposed to the rays. But

German surgeon Theodor Billroth was the first to employ anesthesia and antiseptic surgical techniques, which made it possible to battle cancer in the operating room.

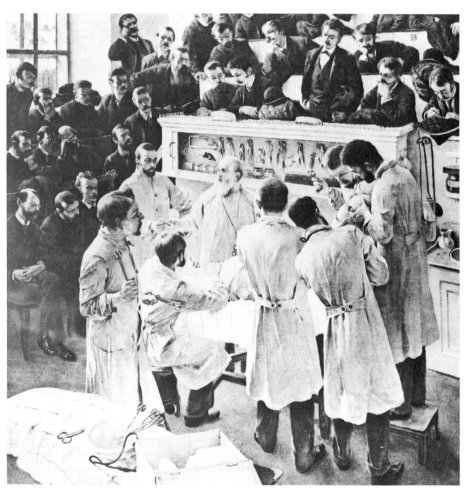

Marie Curie, along with her husband, Pierre, isolated radium, the radio-active source of the first X rays, in 1898.

to a few physicians with imagination the idea occurred that these effects might be harnessed to destroy cancer cells. If radiation could harm normal tissue, they asked, could it also harm cancer? By the early 1900s, doctors were using X rays and gamma rays, the rays emitted by radium, to treat cancer.

Today, many cancer patients are still treated with gamma rays or with rays released by artificial radioactive sources such as cobalt-60, gold-198, cesium-137, or phosphorus-32. Newer forms of radiation come from neutrons and more rapidly moving atomic particles that focus the rays with a diamond cutter's precision.

During the 1940s, physicists discovered and harnessed other rays—high-energy pieces of smashed atoms that had many of the same destructive effects as X rays and gamma rays. Today, streams of nuclear particles, including pions, protons, and neutrons, generated by such complex atom-smashing machines as cyclotrons and linear accelerators, are sometimes used to alter and destroy the genetic material (the DNA and RNA) inside cancer cells. These beams, and those that narrowly focus X rays and gamma rays, can prevent the cancer cells from dividing and reproducing, with very little damage to nearby normal cells.

Doctors who specialize in cancer radiation—called radiation oncologists—use computers to measure the length and depth of a beam as precisely as possible. Molds and casts made of metals that block radiation are tailor-made to protect healthy tissue from the unwanted rays during treatment.

To reduce the amount of radiation needed to eliminate cancer cells, radiation oncologists can in some cases increase the target cells' sensitivity to radiation by using heat or drugs. Other cancers, such as small cancers of the lip and tongue, are so naturally sensitive to radiation that such additional methods are unnecessary. *Radiotherapy* is also effective in controlling symptoms and pain in patients with widespread, incurable cancer. For example, radiation cannot kill all the cancer cells in a patient whose cancer has spread to the bones, but it can kill enough to eliminate pain and give the patient months or even years to live.

Radiation is not without side effects. In fact, ironically, radiation is in itself carcinogenic, or cancer causing. People undergoing radiation therapy may suffer mild burns, develop some scarring, and experience temporary hair loss, dryness of the mouth, and fluctuations in blood pressure. Most patients, however, feel completely well and normal again within a month or two after treatment. New machines and expertise have greatly reduced the worst side effects, and by all accounts the benefits of radiation outweigh the side effects.

Radiation treatment involves many steps; this electronic simulator helps localize the tumor before therapy begins.

CHEMOTHERAPY

Cancers that have spread to distant parts of the body or that are widespread from the moment they arise—leukemias, for example—usually cannot be cured or controlled with radiation, surgery, or even a combination of the two. The third major type of treatment to be developed, chemical therapy (chemotherapy for short), is the preferred means of attacking such cancers because chemicals circulate body wide. The systemic nature of chemotherapy is different from the targeted, selective, regional nature of radiation and surgery.

Cancer-killing drugs are responsible for the dramatic cure rates in many childhood cancers, such as leukemia. They are the first line of treatment in 15% of all cancers and are used in combination with surgery and radiation in perhaps half of all cancers.

It was not until the middle of this century that scientists discovered chemicals that could alter cancer cells in a predictable and consistent way without also killing the host organism. The modern age of chemotherapy began in 1941, when Dr. Charles Huggins discovered that the female sex hormone estrogen could decrease the size of prostate cancers in men. The drug eliminated the patients' pain almost instantly. Dr. Huggins eventually earned a Nobel Prize for his finding. A year later, chemotherapy development got another major boost when researchers discovered that mechlorethamine, the active ingredient in a chemical-warfare weapon called mustard gas, greatly reduced the size of lymph-gland tumors. In 1943, autopsies of more than 80 men exposed to mustard gas when a cargo ship was bombed showed that their blood contained very few white cells, which help fight infections. (White cells are among the most rapidly dividing cells in the body.) As soon as World War II ended the secrecy surrounding such study results, doctors began to build on the idea that if mechlorethamine was most effective in killing rapidly dividing cells and if cancer is characterized by rapid cell division, would not this drug—and drugs like it—be an effective cancer therapy? The answer was yes, and that drug is still in use today, in conjunction with radiation treatment, to treat Hodgkin's disease, which is a type of cancer of the lymph nodes.

In another major step, it was discovered that leukemia developed most readily in mice with rich supplies of a vital body chemical called folic acid. Scientists reasoned that if they could find an anti-folic-acid drug, they might successfully treat leukemia. The drug found was *methotrexate*, which continues to be the chemical foundation of chemotherapy for children with acute leukemia.

Today, oncologists have access to dozens of drugs that fall into five main categories:

- Alkylating agents that bond to DNA and RNA (ribonucleic acid) and sabotage cancer-cell messages that direct growth. These include Cytoxan, L-PAM, Myleran, BCNU, and Mustargen (mechlorethamine hydrochloride).

- *Antimetabolites* that kill cancer cells by introducing a "ringer" substance that mimics the substances that cells need to grow but is not quite effective at actually meeting the cells' requirements. These include methotrexate, 5-fluorouracil, and cytosine arabinoside.

- Antibiotics made from certain fungus growths that work something like alkylating agents. These include Adriamycin, daunomycin, and bleomycin.

- Plant alkaloids that prevent cell division without using the ringer products. These include vincristine and vinblastine.

- Natural and man-made hormones that stimulate or slow down the rate at which cancer cells grow and mature. These include prednisone, tamoxifen citrate, and estrogen compounds.

Patients can often get chemotherapy in a doctor's office or the outpatient department of a hospital's cancer clinic. The drugs are given by pill or by injection into a vein or muscle. The key strategy in chemotherapy is to hit the largest number of cancer cells when they are most vulnerable (during division, for example) with the highest dose of the most potent drug possible without overwhelming the body's normal cells and activities.

Medical oncologists know that cancer cells are in some ways like normal cells and that giving toxic drugs is therefore a sensitive balancing act. They know that they must protect normal cells by taking advantage of even the subtlest differences between them and cancer cells when administering the drugs. Or they must somehow rescue normal cells by supporting patients with extra nutrients, antibiotics, and a germ-free environment during and after chemotherapy.

Therapists also know that cancers are not always composed of identical cells. As cancers progress, some cells mutate or alter themselves. These cells go on to become clones, or colonies that may be resistant to drugs. One drug may therefore kill 99.99% of a cancer's cells. But that one-tenth of 1% that is resistant can go on to repopulate the whole tumor. Because cancers typically contain millions of cells, even a "kill ratio" of 99.99% can leave thousands of cells behind. That is why chemotherapists generally use drugs in combination. If several drugs are given, chances are better that cells missed by one will be destroyed by another. The standard chemotherapy for Hodgkin's disease, for instance, is known as MOPP: Mustargen, Oncovin (vincristine sulfate), prednisone, and procarbazine hydrochloride.

By the end of the 1980s it is estimated that drugs will cure or substantially prolong the life of more than half of all patients with the following cancers: acute lymphoblastic leukemia, Burkitt's lymphoma, childhood lymphoma, embryonal cell cancer, gestational trophoblastic cancer, Hodgkin's disease, neuroblastoma, testicular cancer, and Wilms' tumor.

There is a downside to chemotherapy, however, just as there is to radiation. Because chemicals used to treat cancer are in effect cell poisoners, they sometimes violently disrupt the body's normal metabolic rhythms and irritate fragile tissues in the lining of the digestive tract, the skin, and other organs. Thus, some anticancer drugs make patients feel nauseous and feverish. They can also cause hair loss, create temporary sores in the mouth, and cause diarrhea. Most drugs suppress bone marrow growth, where red blood cells, platelets, and white cells are made; this

Dr. Harry Brem of Johns Hopkins University Hospital in Baltimore, Maryland, holds a polymer wafer that, once implanted, allows for the slow release of cancer-fighting chemicals near the site in this patient's head where a malignant tumor was removed.

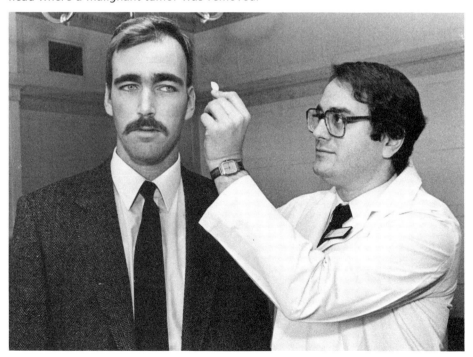

can make a person prone to serious infections. Other drugs can cause nerve damage, sterility, and, in some cases, other kinds of cancer.

Despite this list of problems, it is not true that all patients receiving chemotherapy get very sick. Side effects vary greatly and depend on the kind of cancer being treated and how responsive the cancer is. Even two people with the same cancer who receive the same treatment may differ enormously in the type and intensity of side effects they suffer. Moreover, doctors now have other medicines and psychotherapies that help patients get through the worst times. Even though the three most significant cancer therapies have undergone vast improvements since their development, many patients are frightened to undergo treatment and to suffer the potential side effects. It is essential, however, that all cancer patients immediately seek whatever form of therapy their disease requires, because the best chance of being cured depends on getting the best treatment at the earliest possible time. The payoff, as millions of cured cancer patients can attest, is worth it: longer and better lives.

•   •   •   •

CHAPTER 6

• • • • • • • • • • • • • •

YOUNG PEOPLE
WITH CANCER

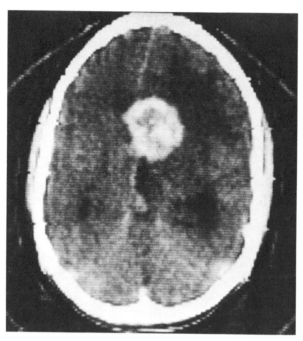

A brain tumor. Cancers of the brain are among the more common forms of the disease among children.

Few diagnoses are as devastating as that of cancer in children and teenagers. These young people, who should have all of life before them, must deal not only with the possibility of suffering and dying but also with the sabotage of life's basic plan. Moreover, whereas an adult can try to understand the process of the disease and the therapies used to treat it from an intellectual standpoint, it is often impossible for small children to cope with the unexpected and undeserved pain of both cancer and its treatment.

Although cancer is primarily a disease of older age, it is the major cause of death by disease in children between the ages of

3 and 14. According to the American Cancer Society, an estimated 6,600 American children each year—most of them preschoolers—are diagnosed with cancers of the blood and bone marrow, bone, lymph nodes, brain, nervous system, kidneys, and muscle and other soft tissue. Another 1,800 children die each year of cancer, about half from leukemia, the most common childhood cancer. Unlike many adult cancers, most childhood cancers cannot be prevented. They may be inherited or emerge very early in childhood.

Because its symptoms are often extremely subtle, childhood cancer is often difficult to detect. A loss of energy, paleness, or

These Florida schoolchildren made a commitment toward a healthy future by declaring themselves "smoke free."

fever can be symptoms of other, far less dangerous illnesses. Only when symptoms persist and become more severe are tests performed. The most serious of these more advanced symptoms include an unusual mass or swelling anywhere in the body that is not due to a known cause such as a fall; unexplained paleness and loss of energy; pain, especially in the legs, that does not go away; long bouts of fever not associated with flu or other infections; a sudden loss or blurring of vision; and a sudden loss of weight.

Only 1% of the known types of cancer is likely to strike children and adolescents. One attempt to differentiate the cancers children are prone to from those that affect only adults has to do with two of the three layers of the fetal embryo: the mesoderm and the endoderm. (The third layer is the ectoderm.) The connective tissues, bone and cartilage, as well as blood, blood vessels, and lymphoid organs are all derived from the mesodermic layer, as are the kidney and gonads. The cancers corresponding to these areas are leukemia, kidney cancer, or Wilms' tumor, and osteogenic sarcoma, among others. Adults are more prone than children to cancers of the respiratory and digestive tract, both of which develop from the endoderm. Cancers that strike organs from these areas—such as the lungs or colon—are often prodded by such factors as cigarette smoke and poor dietary habits.

PRINCIPLE CHILDHOOD CANCERS

The most common form of childhood cancer is leukemia. It usually strikes children under the age of 10 in an acute form, marked by rapid onset. Millions of abnormal white blood cells, which arise in the bone marrow, flow into the bloodstream, crowding out normal white cells that produce antibodies to fight infection, platelets that control bleeding, and red cells that supply oxygen to the body. Tests for childhood leukemia include blood counts, removal and examination of bone marrow, studies of blood cells, and biopsy. Such treatments as blood transfusions, antibiotics, chemotherapy, and bone marrow transplants have raised the survival rate of children with acute lymphocytic leukemia from less than 5% in the 1950s to up to 75% in 1989.

Two bone cancers that affect children, osteogenic sarcoma and Ewing's sarcoma, begin with swelling of surrounding tissue. These diseases are usually detected by bone X rays, CAT scans (computerized axial tomography of the brain and spinal cord), and biopsy. Surgery combined with radiation therapy has proved to be a moderately successful treatment for both cancers, and the 5-year survival rate for young victims is roughly 50%.

The most common soft-tissue cancer found in children is called rhabdomyosarcoma, which usually arises in the head, neck, genital area, trunk, arms, or legs. Tests for this disease include X rays, bone and liver scans, bone marrow biopsy, and intravenous pyelogram, or IVP (an examination of the ureter and the pelvic lining). Rhabdomyosarcoma is treated with surgery, followed by both radiation therapy and chemotherapy. Retinoblastoma is an inherited eye disease (see Chapter 2) that usually strikes children four years old or younger. Eye examinations, X rays, CAT scans, and examinations of bone marrow and spinal fluid can test for this disease, and with early detection and prompt treatment—through surgery and radiation therapy—cure is likely.

The most common brain cancers are neuroblastoma and glioblastoma, both of which are characterized in early stages by such symptoms as dizziness, headaches, blurred vision, nausea, and problems with walking and balance. Like retinoblastoma, these cancers affect children who are usually of preschool age or younger. Detection procedures for neuroblastoma and glioblastoma include IVP, blood tests, urine tests, and biopsy. Treatment, which entails surgery followed by chemotherapy and radiation therapy, is effective: More than half of all children with neuroblastoma and glioblastoma (as well as other forms of brain cancer) survive at least five years.

Wilms' tumor is usually suspected when there is a lump in the abdomen. It is detected by X ray, urinalysis, IVP, CAT scan, ultrasound, and liver and bone scans. More than 80% of patients who receive proper treatment—surgery followed by either radiation therapy or chemotherapy—reach the 5-year survival plateau.

One of the most promising developments since the advent of radiation therapy has been the dramatic increase in the survival rate of children with Hodgkin's disease and lymphoma. These are cancers that form in the lymph nodes and are characterized by swelling of the lymph glands in the armpit, neck, or groin. They often invade the bone marrow and other organs, making the patient feel weak and feverish. These cancers can be detected through blood tests, X rays, bone marrow removal and examination, CAT scan, and biopsy. Owing to the combination treatment of radiation and chemotherapy, the 5-year survival rate for Hodgkin's disease and non-Hodgkin's lymphomas detected in early stages is 88%.

PSYCHOLOGICAL ASPECTS

Because the three main cancer therapies have diminished the death rate for childhood cancer so dramatically, the issue for many children and young teenagers with cancer is no longer dying of the disease but living with it. Of course this is a blessing, but the strain of living as a cancer survivor can make the natural emotional obstacles of adolescence and growing up that much harder to deal with. The period of struggling with self-image, career development, family, friends, and (later) love, courtship, and marriage can be much more difficult for people with cancer. They are forced to delay—sometimes for years—the chance to participate in normal adolescent and young-adult activities. Symptoms of the illness and side effects of treatment keep patients out of school and prevent them from attending social events for long periods of time. Often the patients' appearance will be affected by hair loss, weight loss, and surgical scars. In addition, there can be persistent fear and anxiety over the presence of the disease, primarily because 10% of child survivors will develop a second cancer within 20 years. Although that means 90% will not, the possibility is haunting.

Society still discriminates—sometimes without realizing it—against people who are ill, especially with a life-threatening disease. "Beyond the aura of risk always hanging over them, they face huge difficulties getting good jobs, getting into good schools and developing careers," says Dr. Brigid Leventhal, a childhood cancer specialist at Johns Hopkins University Hospital who has treated many hundreds of young patients successfully. Prospective employers and admissions officers in professional schools, she says, worry that their investment in job training or education will not pay off because the patients will succumb to their disease or have to take too much time off for treatment. In addition, she notes, "the drugs they have to take may produce wide swings of mood and unlovely behavior, for which they blame themselves. Family and friends and teachers often don't understand."

Doctors and other professionals are now paying more attention to the young cancer patients' psychological and social needs. "Kids today are being cured of the diseases, but they're not always left physically and psychologically intact," noted Dr. Aaron Rausen, a child-cancer specialist at New York University Medical Center. "Now we're trying to handle the problems associated with treatments, for the kids and their family."

Psychologists like James Harris at Johns Hopkins are studying the effects of anticancer drugs on mood and behavior. And they are adding psychological counseling, group therapy, and psychotropic, or mood-altering, drugs to their arsenal of anticancer weapons. "Just being able to tell kids that their behavior problems are not their fault, that the drugs are to blame, is reassuring," says Harris. Teenagers and young adults are also encouraged to talk to their family and friends about their fears, to form support groups for social activities, and to recruit such techniques as meditation and biofeedback to help control anxiety and pain.

Child psychologists are working to reduce pain associated with cancer testing and treatment, pain that interferes with the willingness of children and their families to go along with remedies that can save their life. Parents can and should be taught to help reduce their children's anxiety over treatments.

It is also not uncommon for the victim to experience several unpleasant emotional reactions to his or her situation. Social workers have reported that children often experience intense guilt over their condition, which they somehow perceive as being a punishment for some conceived wrong. In such cases, the parents' help is elicited in getting the child to air his or her feelings so as to dispel the irrational basis of those feelings.

Better artificial limbs, plastic surgery, psychotherapy to improve body image, and better educational opportunities are helping thousands of long-term cancer survivors lead a higher-quality life. For example, artificial limbs, called prostheses, are light-

Ted Kennedy, Jr.

"When I injured my leg, it hurt for an abnormal period of time," wrote Ted Kennedy, Jr., in *People* magazine in April 1978. "I finally went to Georgetown University Hospital for a diagnosis. That's where they told me they'd have to remove part of my leg . . . it was such a strange type of cancer."

It was cancer of the cartilage, below his right knee. That was in 1973, when Kennedy, the son of Edward Kennedy, Democratic senator from Massachusetts, was a 12-year-old seventh grader at St. Alban's School in Washington, D.C. The amputation was followed by a series of chemotherapy treatments that, Kennedy writes, "were gruesome. You lose all your hair, you vomit for about four days straight, you can't keep anything down. You lose weight and you feel just terrible."

After the operation, he was fitted with a prosthesis called a CAT-CAM (Contoured Abducted Trochanteric Controlled Alignment Method), which was developed by John Sabolich of Oklahoma City. With earlier prostheses, a patient's pelvic bone rested in a socket, leaving the stump free to drift out. This made it difficult to sit down and uncomfortable to walk. The CAT-CAM holds the hip, thigh, and pelvis in proper alignment and makes it possible for the wearer to take natural strides.

Once prepared, Kennedy wasted no time trying his artificial limb out on ski slopes, water skis, and squash courts.

Before he was physically outfitted, however, Kennedy had to prepare himself emotionally. "One thing you obviously start asking youself is, 'Why me?' I mean, why did it have to happen to me out of all the people in the world? Are any girls ever going to go out with me? Will people look at me the same? Then I said to myself: You've just got to face up to these questions."

The Kennedy family tradition leaves little room for self-pity. Their commitment to public service was exemplified by John F. Kennedy, the 35th president of the United States, and Kennedy has not only cited his uncle's heritage as a source of emotional strength but has followed in its path by acting as a spokesman for the disabled, representing their interests at congressional hearings on bills to assist them with paternal leave, housing, and transportation. He also started a nonprofit organization, now defunct, called Facing the Challenge, which advocated the rights of the disabled. "He has the potential," said Liz Savage, a spokesperson for the Epilepsy Foundation of America, "to become the Martin Luther King of the disability community."

weight, flexible, and lifelike; many young victims of bone cancer who have undergone amputations now ski, swim, hike, climb mountains, dance, play basketball, and ride bicycles. Plastic surgeons are using silicone implants and new skin-grafting techniques to replace lost tissue, remove scars, and restore skin so that cancer patients look good to themselves and others.

In Connecticut, actor Paul Newman has established The Hole in the Wall Gang Camp for young people with cancer and other blood diseases. Named for the gang made famous in the 1969 Paul Newman–Robert Redford film *Butch Cassidy and the Sundance Kid*, the 300-acre camp is a sports and recreation center for young people, who are also supervised by volunteer doctors and nurses and the chief pediatrician at Yale New Haven Hospital.

Actor Paul Newman used the profits from sales of products derived from his personal recipes to found the Hole in the Wall Gang Camp for children with cancer.

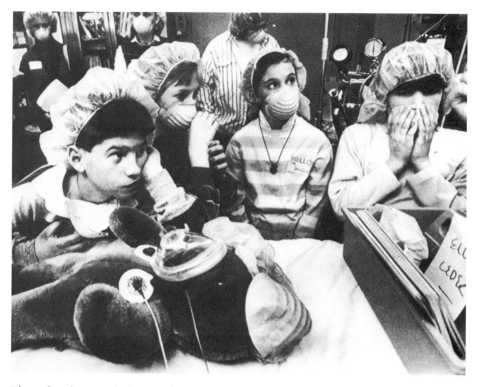

These brothers and sisters of young cancer patients were invited to the Floating Hospital for Children in Boston to witness the treatments—here performed on a teddy bear—that their siblings must endure.

Many support groups that help families who have children with cancer have sprung up to provide emotional guidance and a chance to talk out problems and to protect the social and legal rights of cancer patients and cancer survivors. The New England Medical Center's Floating Hospital for Children, for example, has a program that helps the brothers and sisters of young cancer patients, siblings who often feel anxious, lonely, and angry over the attention their sick brothers and sisters receive. The American Cancer Society has lists, with addresses, of other family-support groups in local communities.

Support groups and psychological counseling are a significant part of the recovery process and have vastly improved the quality of young cancer patients' lives. But even more important has been the advent of medical treatment. Since the 1950s, surgery, radiation therapy, and chemotherapy have more than doubled the survival rate of young cancer victims, an achievement of no small proportion. "To save the life of an adult cancer patient is to save perhaps a decade or two," noted one oncologist. "To save the life of a child with cancer is to save a lifetime."

●   ●   ●   ●

CHAPTER 7

TREATING AND CURING CANCER: NEW STRATEGIES

The sad story of
MY FATHER'S GREAT SUFFERING
FROM **CANCER**
Read the following and be convinced
WE CAN CURE YOU.

Forty-five years ago my father who was himself a doctor, had a vicious cancer that was eating away his life. The best physicians in America could do nothing for him. After nine long years of awful suffering, and after the cancer had totally eaten away his nose and portions of his face (as shown in his picture here given) his palate was entirely destroyed together with portions of his throat. Father fortunately discovered the great remedy that cured him. This was over forty years ago, and he has never suffered a day since.

This same discovery has now cured thousands who were threatened with operation and death. And to prove that this is the truth we will give their sworn statement if you will write us. Doctors, Lawyers, Mechanics, Ministers, Laboring Men, Bankers and all classes recommend this glorious life-saving discovery, and we want the whole world to benefit by it.

HAVE YOU CANCER, Tumors, Ulcers, Abscesses, Fever Sores, Goitre, Catarrh, Salt-Rheum, Rheumatism, Piles, Eczema, Scald Head or Scrofula in any form.

We positively guarantee our statements true, perfect satisfaction and honest service—or money refunded.

It will cost you nothing to learn the truth about this wonderful home treatment without the knife or caustic. And if you know anyone who is afflicted with any disease above mentioned, you can do them a Christian act of kindness by sending us their addresses so we can write them how easily they can be cured in their own home. This is no idle talk, we mean just what we say. We have cured others, and can cure you. Forty years experience guarantees success. Write us today; delay is dangerous. Illustrated Booklet FREE.

DRS. MIXER, 286 State St., HASTINGS, MICH.

There have been many spurious
claims of cancer cures.

When the parents of seven-year-old Grace were told that their daughter, who had a lump in her abdomen and a constant fever, had cancer, they were understandably distraught. They were further frightened when they learned that she would need surgery, radiation, and chemotherapy. Then the pediatric oncologist gently explained that there was less than a 50-50 chance their daughter would live, even after the treatments.

Soon after, a relative of Grace's parents told them about a doctor in a nearby state who could cure their daughter without surgery, radiation, or chemotherapy. The "treatment" consisted of some vitamin pills and a special diet. It cost a great deal of money, the parents were told, but was it not worth it?

For several months, Grace took the pills and followed the special diet. At the beginning of the treatment, the family was filled with hope, and Grace actually seemed to feel better for a while.

But soon she became more tired. The lumps in her abdomen grew bigger, and she had a fever almost constantly. One night she was so sick that her parents took her to the emergency room of the community hospital. The next day, the pediatric oncologist was called in. The cancer, rhabdomyosarcoma, had spread. Surgery would no longer be possible. They started Grace on chemotherapy, which made her feel better for the few months until she died.

Grace's tragic story happens all too often in the United States. Fear and misunderstanding of cancer and its treatments lead many people to seek unorthodox, unproved treatments because they promise cures without side effects. In other cases, cancer treatments do fail, the cancer recurs, and desperate families and friends seek help from any source that promises to save or extend life.

Many unproved cancer remedies are dangerous, outright frauds, offered by people who simply wish to make money and do not care that the time and money cancer patients spend on phony therapies often ruins their chance for a real cure. In other situations, therapists may truly believe their treatment helps, but the drugs or diets have never been submitted to or passed rigorous scientific testing. Still other treatments have some value but are limited, risky, and unpredictable.

Patients are especially vulnerable to outlandish claims when surgery, radiation, and chemotherapy have failed to cure or control cancer. Among the most popular quack treatments in recent years have been laetrile, a compound made from apricot pits and sometimes called amygdalin, or vitamin B_{17}; megavitamin therapy, which consists of massive doses of vitamins; and enemas that are supposed to "purge" the cancer from the body.

None of these treatments work. Their perpetrators, however, generally claim that they have not been fairly tested or that the medical "establishment" has a vested interest in keeping their

These patients are flying to Mexico to receive laetrile after the so-called treatment was banned in America.

successes quiet. One thing all such treatments have in common is that they are costly. Even worse, they delay or prevent treatments that can really help.

NEW TREATMENTS

It is important to realize, however, that there are cancer treatments besides surgery, radiation, and traditional chemotherapy that are neither quackery nor unproven. Scientists are working on new treatments every day and attempting to refine old ones.

These treatments are based on experimental drugs and on new strategies that have emerged as scientists have learned more about the biology of cancer.

These new treatments are often full of hope and promise. But they are not always available to all cancer patients, because they must still be studied under very controlled conditions to ensure

The National Cancer Institute has sponsored a five-year effort to gather plant specimens from jungles. Pictured is a dried rosy periwinkle plant, which has been used to make vincristine and vinblastine, two leukemia-fighting drugs.

that they work without hurting patients. Or they may still be in the early stages of development and testing and are not yet ready for use in humans.

IMMUNOTHERAPY

One of the most promising new forms of cancer treatment is immunotherapy, which has long been a dream of cancer specialists. Their hope is that if they can orchestrate the body's own defenses—especially disease-fighting antibodies—they can turn on or turn up the search for stray cancer cells and clean up tumor-cell clones that have escaped the three major cancer therapies. The faith in immunotherapy is based on the idea that the human immune system is always working to protect the body against cancer. Experiments have shown that normal cells are continuously transformed into cancer cells in small numbers, and the accepted theory is that the immune system monitors these isolated tumors and eradicates them in most cases long before they take root.

Harnessing the body's methods, scientists believe, not only will be safer than drugs, surgery, and radiation but is probably the only way to ferret out the most drug-resistant and hidden of cancer's "strays," the metastases that change their own nature to become resistant and escape destruction by drugs or radiation.

One way scientists have tried to enlist the immune response in the fight against cancer is to stimulate the whole system at once. For example, it is well known that when a person gets a bacterial infection—for example, strep throat or flu—his or her body launches a whole array of chemicals and special white blood cells to fight off the invader. Could the body launch that array when it is needed to fight cancer?

Efforts to do this with vaccines made of germs and other agents generally have not worked. The stimulation was too general, too short-lived, and often too toxic. But in the 1960s and 1970s scientists began to understand that cancer cells triggered a variety

Immunotherapy is a type of cancer treatment that uses natural or man-made substances to stimulate the body's immune system, usually repressed by the cancer, to fight disease. One such treatment is Interleuken-2, which stimulates the growth of lymphocytes.

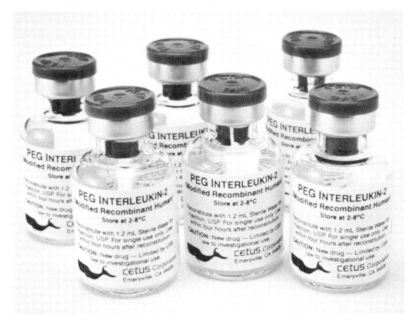

of immune responses that were quite specific and that these re-actions often unleashed one or more of a half-dozen hormonelike molecules from the thymus gland, spleen, bone marrow, and lymph glands, along with a network of special antibody cells. All were able to fight cancer cells.

The more the scientists discovered about this specific immune system, the more complicated it became. Both the difficulty and fundamental value of this work was underscored in 1987 when Dr. Susumu Tonegawa of the Massachusetts Institute of Technology earned a Nobel Prize for discovering how such a limited number of cells could react to so many different foreign proteins (including cancer cells).

Once scientists began to understand the immune system's antibodies—their maneuvers and their suppliers—they began to work on ways to direct these forces to fight cancer. The challenge became one of finding ways to magnify or increase the firepower of the antibodies.

One method that has been the subject of intense investigation is the use of large numbers of pure, genetically engineered antibodies called monoclonal antibodies. They are made by injecting cancer cells from a particular patient into an animal, waiting while the animal's white blood cells form antibodies to the cancer cells, then extracting from the animal's blood those antibodies that react to cancer cells. These antibodies are then fused to a cancer cell in special test tubes, creating a hybridoma that is directed specifically against a particular kind of cancer. The idea, therefore, is to send these created antibodies into the patient's blood to kill the cancer cells from which they were originally bred.

Unfortunately, monoclonal antibodies thus far have not had tremendous success battling cancer tumors. Some victories were reported, including the cure of a lymphoma patient by Ronald Levy at Stanford University in 1981, but all in all the record has been one of defeat. Researchers came to agree that monoclonal antibodies alone cannot eradicate a cancer, partly because their effect is not powerful enough, and partly because they are aimed at what is in effect a moving target. Cancer antigens can change subtly enough to evade attack by a monoclonal antibody, and even if some cells are destroyed, others appear with different antigens.

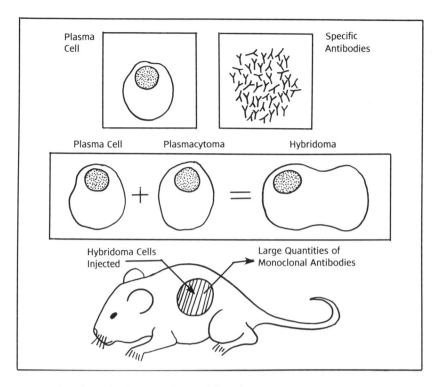

Plasma Cell

Specific Antibodies

Plasma Cell   Plasmacytoma   Hybridoma

Hybridoma Cells Injected

Large Quantities of Monoclonal Antibodies

Monoclonal antibodies are formed first by injecting an animal with a substance that will cause the formation of antibodies. The plasma cells that produced these are then in turn fused with cancer cells called myelomas, which confer on the resulting hybrids the ability to continue growing indefinitely. These hybridomas in turn produce the monoclonal antibodies that stimulate the immune system to fight cancer.

Researchers have since experimented with combining monoclonal antibodies with different toxic chemicals to be released when the antibody reaches a cancer cell. Some researchers attach anticancer drugs, some use radioactive isotopes, and some use ricin, a toxin that penetrates a cancer cell and kills it. The success rate of this method has yet to be determined.

Another immunotherapeutic strategy scientists are studying is the use of biological response modifiers, or BRMs, which have the ability to stimulate or slow down all growth. These include natural substances such as interferons (molecules that prevent viruses from reproducing outside infected cells) and interleukin-2 (a molecule that helps direct and regulate immune-system function). Scientists are also trying to harness the immune system by finding biochemical "switches" that safely turn on or off natural controls of the system. So far, immunotherapies have proven of limited value, but many scientists believe that they may form the basis for a whole new generation of anticancer drugs.

BONE MARROW TRANSPLANTS

Another new form of anticancer treatment is the bone marrow transplant. This approach is most often used in patients with advanced leukemia who have failed to respond to chemotherapy. The object of bone marrow transplants is to replace the patient's damaged blood-forming tissues—the tissues that produce cancerous blood cells—with normal marrow. This must be done by first killing all or most of a patient's own marrow with high doses of drugs, then transplanting marrow from a closely related or matched donor. This procedure is very risky. The problem is not that the transplanted cells may be rejected but rather that they will reject the rest of the body's tissue.

Studies have shown that a rejection is less likely to occur when donor and patient are genetically matched and particularly when certain proteins in the white blood cells are the same for both donor and recipient. Therefore, the ideal donor is an identical twin, whose genes are exact duplicates of those of the patient. Other family members may also be good candidates; there is a 25% chance that any one sister or brother has proteins that are genetically identical to that of the patient.

Before the bone marrow transplant procedure begins, the patient is given both radiation and chemotherapy treatments to prevent the immune system from initially rejecting the transplanted matter and to kill cancer cells both in the marrow and throughout the body. Once the donor's marrow is injected into the patient, it travels through the blood and then enters the marrow through cavities in the bones. If the transplant is successful, the number of platelets and granulocytes in the patient's blood will rise significantly. The transplanted bone marrow will probably not begin producing new blood cells until two to four weeks after the procedure is completed.

When successful, bone marrow transplants have proved to be an effective treatment for leukemia. Scientists are currently em-

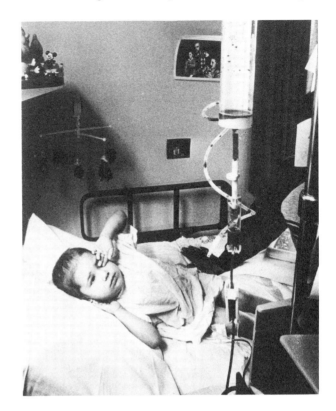

This girl, suffering from retinoblastoma, has just received a bone marrow transplant from her sister.

ploying new techniques that would make it possible for a non-related donor to be used and are even investigating the possibility of starting a donor bank to collect marrow samples from the general population.

HELPING PATIENTS COPE

Contemporary scientists know that psychological and social factors make a real difference in how well cancer treatments work. And social workers, psychologists, and psychiatrists are now often a standard part of the cancer-treatment team.

For example, by treating patients with anxiety-relieving drugs, doctors can keep many more of them from dropping out of potentially lifesaving treatments that create anxiety and aggravate the nausea and illness that accompany the treatment.

Child psychologists are learning to use medicines, hypnosis, meditation, behavior modification, and psychotherapy to reduce the pain associated with cancer treatment. Drugs are also available to help restore appetite. These treatments are used for the benefit of the parents as well as for the children. If parents must see their children suffer with every treatment session, they are less likely to keep appointments and more likely to seek quacks.

"The goal," says Dr. Robert O. Pasnau, former president of the American Psychiatric Association, "is to integrate the biological, psychological, and social needs of the patient."

Another goal is to continue educating people about the facts and nature of cancer. Many people still view the disease as a "rotting away" of the body's deepest organs, as an unpredictable, uncontrollably painful way to die. Doctors still write about "cancerophobia" as a disease in itself, and as the writer Susan Sontag has noted, cancer is still often described as an insurgent, colonizing, relentless enemy; the effort to stop it is described by Sontag as a military action involving "cell kills" and "bombardments." It is no accident that the descriptions often read like battlefield reports.

Some experts today believe that a new metaphor may be in order. The disease is still a major threat to life and health, but it is far less of a juggernaut than it was just a decade ago. Like other subjects of scientific research, cancer's basic nature—its exotic and precise ability to transform cells—is a source of some wonder. More to the point, science is beginning to understand it. And with this understanding has come more effective treatments, the development of exciting experimental therapies, and higher incidences of cure.

•   •   •   •

APPENDIX:
FOR MORE INFORMATION

The following is a list of organizations and associations that can provide further information about cancer.

GENERAL INFORMATION

American Cancer Society
1599 Clifton Road, N.E.
Atlanta, GA 30329
(404) 320-3333

The Candlelighters Childhood
  Cancer Foundation
2025 I Street, N.W.
Washington, DC 20006
(202) 659-5136

National Cancer Institute
National Institutes of Health
9000 Rockville Pike, Building 31,
  10A24
Bethesda, MD 20892
(301) 496-5583

National Cancer Institute of Canada
401-77 Bloor Street West
Toronto, Ontario M5S 2V7
Canada
(416) 961-7223

HOSPICES

National Hospice Organization
1311A Dolley Madison Boulevard
Suite 3B
McLean, VA 22101
(703) 356-6770

Ronald McDonald House
National Coordinator
500 North Michigan Avenue
Chicago, IL 60611
(312) 836-7129

HOT LINES

Cancer Information and Counseling
  Hot Line
Operated by the American Medical
  Center
(Denver, CO)
(800) 525-3777

Cancer Information Hot Line
Breast Examination Hot Line
Operated by the National Cancer
  Institute
(800) 4-CANCER
(9:00 A.M.–4:30 P.M.)
(800) 638-6694
(24 hours a day)
(800) 638-6070 (Alaska)
(202) 636-5700 (District of
  Columbia, Maryland, and
  Virginia suburbs)
(800) 524-1234 (Hawaii, Number 6;
  Oahu, neighboring islands—call
  collect)

Cancer Response Hot Line
Operated by the American Cancer
   Society
(800) ACS-2345

National Second Opinion Hot Line
(800) 638-6833

PSYCHOLOGICAL THERAPY

The following is a list of organizations that provide information and support for both cancer patients and their families. The services offered by these organizations include professional counseling and planning, patient education programs, self-help programs, and group therapy and support groups.

Cancer Care, Inc.
1180 Avenue of the Americas
New York, NY 10036
(212) 221-3300

Cancer Connection
H & R Block Building
4410 Main
Kansas City, MO 64111
(816) 932-8453

Cancer Counseling and Research
   Center
P.O. Box 1055
Azle, TX 76020
(817) 444-4073

Cansurmount
c/o American Cancer Society
1599 Clifton Road, N.E.
Atlanta, GA 30329
(404) 320-3333

I Can Cope
c/o American Cancer Society
1599 Clifton Road, N.E.
Atlanta, GA 30329
(404) 320-3333

International Association of Cancer
   Counselors
Jannus Associates
1800 Augusta Street, Suite 150
Houston, TX 77057
(713) 780-1057

Make Today Count
P.O. Box 222
Osage Beach, MO 65065
(314) 348-1619

We Can Do!
P.O. Box 723
Arcadia, CA 91006
(818) 357-7527

SPECIFIC CANCERS

BRAIN TUMORS

Association for Brain Tumor
   Research
Suite 200
6232 North Pulaski Road
Chicago, IL 60646
(312) 286-5571

BREAST CANCER

American Institute for Cancer
   Research

Department BSE
Washington, DC 20069
For free self-examination kit, send a self-addressed, stamped envelope.

Reach To Recovery
c/o American Cancer Society
1599 Clifton Road, N.E.
Atlanta, GA 30329
(404) 320-3333

DIGESTIVE CANCERS

National Digestive Disease
Education and Information
Clearinghouse
Box NDD1C
Bethesda, MD 20892
(301) 468-6344

LEUKEMIA AND OTHER BLOOD CANCERS

Leukemia Society of America, Inc.
733 Third Avenue
New York, NY 10017
(212) 573-8484

National Heart, Lung and Blood
Institute
National Institutes of Health
Building 31
Room 4A21
Bethesda, MD 20892
(301) 496-4236

National Leukemia Association
Roosevelt Field, Lower Concourse
Garden City, NY 11530
(516) 741-1190

LUNG CANCER

American Lung Association
National Headquarters
1740 Broadway
New York, NY 10019
(212) 325-8700

Spirit and Breath Association
8210 Elmwood Avenue, Suite 209
Skokie, IL 60077
(312) 673-1384

SKIN CANCER

Skin Cancer Foundation
245 Fifth Avenue, Suite 2402
New York, NY 10016
(212) 725-5176

STATE ORGANIZATIONS

The following is a list of the comprehensive and clinical cancer centers and divisions of the American Cancer Society.

ALABAMA

American Cancer Society—
Alabama Division
2926 Central Avenue
Birmingham, AL 35209
(205) 879-2242

Comprehensive Cancer Center
University of Alabama in
Birmingham
University Station
1824 Sixth Avenue, South,
Room 214
Birmingham, AL 35294
(205) 934-5077

ALASKA

American Cancer Society—Alaska
Division

1343 G Street
Anchorage, AK 99501
(907) 277-8696

ARIZONA

American Cancer Society—Arizona
Division
634 West Indian School Road
Phoenix, AZ 85013
(602) 234-3266

University of Arizona Cancer Center
College of Medicine
1501 North Campbell Avenue,
Room 7925
Tucson, AZ 85724
(602) 602-6044

ARKANSAS

American Cancer Society—
Arkansas Division
5520 West Markham Street
Little Rock, AR 72201
(501) 664-3480

CALIFORNIA

American Cancer Society—
California Division
1710 Webster Street
Oakland, CA 94612
(415) 893-7900

Cancer Research Institute
University of Southern California
Comprehensive Cancer Center
P.O. Box 33804
1441 Eastlake Avenue
Los Angeles, CA 90033-0804
(213) 224-6416

COLORADO

American Cancer Society—
Colorado Division
2255 South Oneida
Denver, CO 80224
(303) 758-2030

CONNECTICUT

American Cancer Society—
Connecticut Division
14 Village Lane
Wallingford, CT 06492
(203) 256-7161

Yale University Comprehensive
Cancer Center
333 Cedar Street, Room WWW 205
New Haven, CT 06510
(203) 785-4095

DELAWARE

American Cancer Society—
Delaware Division
1708 Lovering Avenue
Wilmington, DE 19806
(302) 654-6267

DISTRICT OF COLUMBIA

American Cancer Society—District
of Columbia Division
1825 Connecticut Avenue, N.W.
Washington, DC 20009
(202) 483-2600

Vincent T. Lombardi Cancer
Research Center
Georgetown University Medical
Center
3800 Reservoir Road, North West
Washington, DC 20007
(202) 625-2042

FLORIDA

American Cancer Society—Florida
Division
1001 South MacDill Avenue
Tampa, FL 33609
(813) 253-0541

Papanicolaou Comprehensive
Cancer Center
University of Miami Medical School
1475 North West 12th Avenue
P.O. Box 01690 (D8-4)
Miami, FL 33101
(305) 548-4810

GEORGIA

American Cancer Society—Georgia
Division
1422 West Peachtree Street, N.W.
Atlanta, GA 30309
(404) 892-0026

HAWAII

American Cancer Society—Hawaii
Division
200 North Vineyard Boulevard
Honolulu, HI 96817
(808) 531-1662

Cancer Research Center of Hawaii
University of Hawaii at Manoa
1236 Lauhala Street
Honolulu, HI 96813
(808) 548-8415

IDAHO

American Cancer Society—Idaho
    Division
1609 Abbs Street
Boise, ID 83705
(208) 343-4609

ILLINOIS

American Cancer Society—Illinois
    Division
37 South Wabash Avenue
Chicago, IL 60603
(312) 372-0472

Northwestern University Cancer
    Center
Health Sciences Building
303 East Chicago Avenue
Chicago, IL 60611
(312) 908-5250

INDIANA

American Cancer Society—Indiana
    Division
4755 Kingsway Drive
Indianapolis, IN 46205
(317) 257-5326

IOWA

American Cancer Society—Iowa
    Division
Highway 18, West
Mason City, IA 50401
(515) 423-0712

KANSAS

American Cancer Society—Kansas
    Division
3003 Van Buren Street
Topeka, KS 66611
(913) 267-0131

KENTUCKY

American Cancer Society—
    Kentucky Division
1169 Eastern Parkway
Louisville, KY 40217
(502) 459-1867

LOUISIANA

American Cancer Society—
    Louisiana Division
333 Saint Charles Avenue
New Orleans, LA 70130
(504) 523-2029

MAINE

American Cancer Society—Maine
    Division
Federal and Green Streets
Brunswick, ME 04011
(207) 729-3339

MARYLAND

American Cancer Society—
    Maryland Division
200 East Joppa Road
Towson, MD 21204
(301) 828-8890

Johns Hopkins Oncology Center
600 North Wolfe Street, Room 157
Baltimore, MD 21205
(301) 955-8822

MASSACHUSETTS

American Cancer Society—
    Massachusetts Division
247 Commonwealth Avenue
Boston, MA 02116
(617) 267-2650

Dana-Farber Cancer Institute
44 Binney Street
Boston, MA 02115
(617) 732-3636

MICHIGAN

American Cancer Society—
  Michigan Division
1205 East Saginaw Street
Lansing, MI 48906
(517) 371-2920

Meyer L. Prentis Comprehensive
  Cancer Center of Metropolitan
  Detroit
110 East Warren Street
Detroit, MI 48201
(313) 833-1088

MINNESOTA

American Cancer Society—
  Minnesota Division
3316 West 66 Street
Minneapolis, MN 55435
(612) 925-2772

Mayo Comprehensive Cancer
  Center
200 First Street, South West
Rochester, MN 55905
(507) 284-2511

MISSISSIPPI

American Cancer Society—
  Mississippi Division
345 North Mart Plaza
Jackson, MS 39206
(601) 362-8874

MISSOURI

American Cancer Society—
  Missouri Division
3322 American Avenue
Jefferson City, MO 65102
(314) 893-4800

MONTANA

American Cancer Society—
  Montana Division
2820 First Avenue, South
Billings, MT 59101
(406) 252-7111

NEBRASKA

American Cancer Society—
  Nebraska Division
8502 West Center Road
Omaha, NE 68124
(402) 393-5800

NEVADA

American Cancer Society—Nevada
  Division
1325 East Harmon Avenue
Las Vegas, NV 89109
(702) 798-6877

NEW HAMPSHIRE

American Cancer Society—New
  Hampshire Division
686 Mast Road
Manchester, NH 03102
(603) 669-3270

Norris Cotton Cancer Center
Dartmouth-Hitchcock Medical
  Center
Hanover, NH 03755
(603) 646-5505

NEW JERSEY

American Cancer Society—New
  Jersey Division
2600 Route 1, CN2201
North Brunswick, NJ 08902
(201) 297-8000

NEW MEXICO

American Cancer Society—New
  Mexico Division
5800 Lomas Boulevard, N.E.
Albuquerque, NM 87110
(505) 262-2336

NEW YORK

American Cancer Society—Long
  Island Division
535 Broad Hollow Road
Melville, NY 11747
(516) 420-1111

American Cancer Society—New
   York City Division
19 West 56th Street
New York, NY 10019
(212) 586-8700

American Cancer Society—New
   York State Division
6725 Lyons Street
East Syracuse, NY 13057
(315) 437-7025

American Cancer Society—Queens
   Division
111-15 Queens Boulevard
Forest Hills, NY 11375
(212) 263-2224

American Cancer Society—
   Westchester Division
901 North Broadway
White Plains, NY 10603
(919) 949-4800

Memorial Sloan-Kettering Cancer
   Center
1275 York Avenue
New York, NY 10021
(212) 794-6561

NORTH CAROLINA

American Cancer Society—North
   Carolina Division
11 South Boylan Ave
Raleigh, NC 27601
(919) 834-8463

Comprehensive Cancer Center
Duke University Medical Center
227 Jones Building, Research Drive
P.O. Box 3814
Durham, NC 27710
(919) 684-2282

NORTH DAKOTA

American Cancer Society—North
   Dakota Division
115 Roberts Street

Fargo, ND 58102
(701) 232-1385

OHIO

American Cancer Society—Ohio
   Division
1375 Euclid Avenue
Cleveland, OH 44115
(216) 771-6700

Ohio State University
   Comprehensive Cancer Center
410 West 12th Avenue, Suite 302
Columbus, OH 43210
(614) 422-5022

OKLAHOMA

American Cancer Society—
   Oklahoma Division
3800 North Cromwell
Oklahoma City, OK 73112
(405) 946-5000

OREGON

American Cancer Society—Oregon
   Division
0330 Southwest Curry
Portland, OR 97201
(503) 295-6422

PENNSYLVANIA

American Cancer Society—
   Pennsylvania Division
Route 422 and Sipe Avenue
Hershey, PA 17033
(717) 533-6144

American Cancer Society—
   Philadelphia Division
21 South 12th Street
Philadelphia, PA 19107
(215) 665-2900

Fox Chase Cancer Center
7701 Burholme Avenue
Philadelphia, PA 19111
(215) 728-2781

RHODE ISLAND

American Cancer Society—Rhode
  Island Division
345 Blackstone Boulevard
Providence, RI 02906
(401) 831-6970

Roger Williams General Hospital
825 Chalkstone Avenue
Providence, RI 02908
(401) 456-2070

SOUTH CAROLINA

American Cancer Society—South
  Carolina Division
2442 Devine Street
Columbia, SC 29205
(803) 256-0245

SOUTH DAKOTA

American Cancer Society—South
  Dakota Division
1025 North Minnesota Avenue
Sioux Falls, SD 57104
(605) 336-0897

TENNESSEE

American Cancer Society—
  Tennessee Division
713 Melpark Drive
Nashville, TN 37204
(615) 383-1710

St. Jude Children's Research
  Hospital
332 North Lauderdale
Memphis, TN 38101
(901) 522-0301

TEXAS

American Cancer Society—Texas
  Division
3834 Spicewood Springs Road
Austin, TX 78759
(512) 345-4560

UTMB Cancer Center
University of Texas Medical Branch
11th at Mechanic
Microbiology Building
Room 9.104, Route J20
Galveston, TX 77550
(409) 761-2981

UTAH

American Cancer Society—Utah
  Division
610 East South Temple
Salt Lake City, UT 84102
(801) 322-0431

VERMONT

American Cancer Society—
  Vermont Division
13 Loomis Street
Montpelier, VT 05602
(802) 223-2348

Vermont Regional Cancer Center
University of Vermont
1 South Prospect Street
Burlington, VT 05401
(802) 656-4414

VIRGINIA

American Cancer Society—Virginia
  Division
3218 West Cary Street
Richmond, VA 23221
(804) 359-0208

Massey Cancer Center
Medical College of Virginia
Virginia Commonwealth University
MCV Station, Box 37
Richmond, VA 23928
(804) 786-9322

WASHINGTON

American Cancer Society—
  Washington Division
2120 First Avenue, North
Seattle, WA 98109
(206) 283-1152

Fred Hutchinson Cancer Research
  Center
1124 Columbia Street
Seattle, WA 98104
(206) 467-4302

WEST VIRGINIA

American Cancer Society—West
  Virginia Division
240 Capital Street
Charleston, WV 25301
(304) 344-3611

WISCONSIN

American Cancer Society—
  Milwaukee Division
6401 West Capitol Drive
Milwaukee, WI 53216
(414) 461-1100

American Cancer Society—
  Wisconsin Division
615 Sherman Avenue
Madison, WI 53704
(608) 249-0487

University of Wisconsin Clinical
  Cancer Center
600 Highland Avenue
Madison, WI 53792
(608) 263-8610

WYOMING

American Cancer Society—
  Wyoming Division
506 Shoshoni
Cheyenne, WY 82009
(307) 638-3331

FURTHER READING

Ames, Bruce N. "Dietary Carcinogens and Anticarcinogens." *Nature* 221 (September 1983): 1256–62.

Baker, Lynn S. *You and Leukemia*. Philadelphia: Saunders, 1978.

Brody, Jane E., and Arthur I. Holleb, M.D. *You Can Fight Cancer and Win*. New York: Times Books, 1977.

Doll, Richard, and Richard Deto. "The Causes of Cancer: Quantitative Estimates of Avoidable Risks of Cancer in the U.S. Today." *Journal of the National Cancer Institute* 66 (June 1981): 1191–1308.

Dreher, Henry. *Your Defense Against Cancer: The Complete Guide to Cancer Prevention*. New York: Harper & Row, 1989.

Fraumeni, Joseph F., Jr. *Persons at High Risk of Cancer*. Chicago: Academic Press, 1975.

Graham, Jory. *In the Company of Others*. New York: Harcourt Brace Jovanovich, 1982.

Gunther, John. *Death Be Not Proud*. New York: Perennial Library, 1949.

Holleb, Arthur I., M.D. *The American Cancer Society Cancer Book*. New York: Doubleday, 1986.

Kushner, Rose. *Breast Cancer*. New York: Harcourt Brace Jovanovich, 1975.

Le Shan, Lawrence. *Cancer as a Turning Point: A Handbook for People with Cancer, Their Families, and Health Professionals*. New York: Dutton, 1989.

Milan, Albert R., *Breast Self-Examination*. New York: Workman, 1980.

Morra, Marion, and Eve Potts. *Choices: Realistic Alternatives in Cancer*. New York: Avon, 1980.

Pepper, Curtis Bill. *We the Victors: Inspiring Stories of People Who Conquered Cancer and How They Did It*. New York: Doubleday, 1984.

Prada, Luis. "Cancer Facts & Figures—1989." Atlanta: American Cancer Society, 1989.

Rollin, Betty. *First, You Cry*. Philadelphia: Lippincott, 1976.

Rosenbaum, Ernest. *Living With Cancer*. New York: New American Library, 1982.

Shish, Chiaho, Clifford Tabin, and Robert Weinberg. "Human EJ Bladder Carcinoma Oncogene Homologue of Harvey Sarcoma Virus *RAF* Gene." *Nature* 297 (June 1982): 474–78.

Simonton, O. C., and S. Matthews. *Getting Well Again: A Step-by-Step, Self-Help Guide to Overcoming Cancer for Patients and Their Families*. New York: St. Martin's Press, 1978.

Strauss, Linda L. *Coping When a Parent Has Cancer*. New York: Rosen, 1988.

Tucker, Jonathan B. *A Child's Fight Against Leukemia*. New York: Holt, Rinehart and Winston, 1982.

Williams, Chris, and Sue Williams. *Cancer: A Patient's Guide*. New York: Wiley, 1986.

PICTURE CREDITS

GLOSSARY

alkaloid a drug used in cancer treatment to halt growth by preventing cell division; frequently extracted from plants

antibiotic a drug, produced by or derived from a microorganism, that works with the body's immune system to destroy or inhibit the growth of bacteria and to cure illness

antibody one of several types of substances produced by the body to combat bacteria, viruses, or other foreign substances

antigen a bacteria, virus, or other foreign substance that causes the body to form an antibody

antimetabolite a drug used in cancer treatment for its power to replace the essential material of cells

bacteria microscopic unicellular organism; many, but not all, cause disease

benign not recurrent or progressive; opposite of malignant

biopsy excision of tissue from a living organism for examination; performed to detect many forms of cancer

bone marrow transplant a procedure in which the marrow of a healthy donor is injected into the bloodstream of a cancer patient; from the bloodstream it enters the patient's bone cavities; most often used on patients with advanced leukemia

Burkitt's lymphoma a cancer of the lymph system caused by a chromosomal translocation

cancer any malignant tumor that destroys normal tissue as it spreads to adjacent tissue layers or to other parts of the body; a group of more than 100 separate diseases

carcinogen a cancer-causing substance or agent

carcinoma a cancer emerging from cells that line the body's internal or external surfaces; may affect almost any organ or part of the body as it spreads through the bloodstream or lymphatic system

CAT scan computerized axial tomography; a type of diagnostic X ray used to give a three-dimensional picture of the brain and spinal cord; used to detect cancer, usually of the bone

cautery a means of destroying unwanted tissue, such as cancerous tissue, on the body's surface, by the application of an electrically charged burning agent

cell a mass of protoplasm containing a nucleus

chemotherapy the use of drugs or chemicals to treat cancer or to control the growth of cancer cells

chromosomal translocation the accidental movement of genes from one chromosome to another, potentially causing proto-oncogenes to become cancerous

DNA deoxyribonucleic acid; a nucleic acid found mostly in the nuclei of cells; the main carrier of genetic information

Ewing's sarcoma also known as Ewing's tumor; a bone tumor that tends to recur but rarely spreads

genes complex units of chemical material contained within the chromosomes of cells; variations in the patterns formed by the components of genes are responsible for inherited traits

glioblastoma a cell tumor of the neural tissue; occurs chiefly in children

granulocyte a cell found in the blood

Hemoccult a simple test used to detect blood in the stool, which can be a symptom of rectal or bowel cancer

hepatitis viral infection of the liver; infections caused by the hepatitis B virus can lead to liver cancer

Hodgkin's disease a type of cancer characterized by a malignant lymphoma in the lymph glands and spleen

hormone a chemical carried throughout the body in the bloodstream, modifying both structure and function of many bodily processes; certain natural and synthetic hormones are used to slow down cancer growth

hybridoma the fusion of a monoclonal antibody and a cancer cell; specifically designed to destroy cancer cells

immunotherapy a new, relatively unproven form of cancer treatment involving the enhancement of the body's own immune system to battle cancer cells

Kaposi's sarcoma a cancer of the walls of the blood vessels and lymphatic system; once rare, Kaposi's sarcoma is now a common symptom of AIDS

laetrile Vitamin B_{17}; a compound, made from apricot pits, that has been unsuccessfully used in cancer treatment

laser an intensely focused light-amplification device used as a tool in surgery

leukemia a dangerous and often fatal type of cancer caused by the overproduction of white blood cells; the most common form of childhood cancer

lumpectomy excision of a breast tumor followed by radiation

lymphoma a growth of new, and often malignant, tissue in the lymphatic system

malignant likely to infiltrate, spread, and lead to deterioration; malignant tumors are frequently life threatening

mammogram special breast X ray that is used to detect the presence of cancer

mastectomy surgical removal of a breast; one type of breast cancer treatment

mechlorethamine a drug used to kill rapidly dividing cancer cells

melanoma a dangerous, quick-spreading form of skin cancer

metastasis the spreading of cancer in an organism; cancerous colonies (metastases) result from this spreading

metastatic spreading from one area of the body to another; pertaining to bacteria or disease

methotrexate a toxic antimetabolite used in the chemotherapeutic treatment of leukemia

monoclonal antibody a laboratory-made antibody created by extracting the antibodies that an animal has developed after being injected with cancerous cells; used in immunotherapy

mutagen a chemical found in certain foods that has been shown to produce cancer in test animals

neuroblastoma a malignant, hemorrhaging tumor of the brain; occurs chiefly in children

oncogene a gene that has the potential to transform a normal cell into a cancerous one

oncology the study of tumors

organism an individual plant or animal

osteogenic sarcoma osteosarcoma; myelosarcoma; a malignant sarcoma of the bone

palliative surgery surgical reduction of a malignant tumor when a cure is not possible

papilloma a benign tumor of the skin or inner membranes; the papilloma virus may lead to various cancers, including that of the cervix

parasite an organism that relies on another organism for its support or existence, without providing anything useful in return

polyp a swollen and tumorous membrane; found most often in vascular organs such as the nose, colon, intestine, uterus, rectum, and bladder

"primary" cancer a cancerous growth that is confined to one place

proctosigmoidoscopic examination the use of a lighted flexible tube to examine the lining of the bowel; administered to detect rectal and bowel cancer

prostheses artificial devices used as substitutes for body parts that have been amputated, often because of bone cancer

protein a complex molecule consisting of a combination of amino acids

proto-oncogenes healthy genes that eventually become oncogenic; precancerous genes

radiation the emission of penetrating waves or particles, such as light, sound, or radiant heat, used to treat cancer

retinoblastoma a seemingly hereditary form of eye cancer that occurs chiefly in young children

rhabdomyosarcoma rhabdomyoma; a muscular tissue tumor that usually develops in the head, neck, trunk, legs, arms, or genital area

sarcoma a cancer arising from connective tissue such as muscle or bone; may affect the bones, bladder, kidneys, liver, lungs, spleen, and parotids

surgery general term for a manual operation performed to treat or remove an unwanted substance, such as cancer; there are numerous individual types of surgery

T-lymphotropic virus a virus attacking the immune system; HIV, the best known of this kind, is now believed to cause AIDS

toxin a poison produced by bacteria; scientists hope to find and develop toxins that kill cancer cells

tumor an abnormal swelling or growth arising from preexistent cells and serving no useful purpose

vaccine a substance made of killed or weakened bacteria or virus that stimulates the body to create antibodies against the disease caused by that virus or bacteria; these antibodies increase a person's immunity to that particular disease

virus a minute acellular parasite composed of genetic material (either DNA or RNA) and a protein coat; destroys its host cell in order to reproduce

Wilms' tumor a rapidly developing cancer of the kidney; chiefly affects children

INDEX

Joann Ellison Rodgers, M.S. (Columbia), became the deputy director of Public Affairs and director of Media Relations for the Johns Hopkins Medical Institutions in Baltimore, Maryland, in 1984, after 18 years as an award-winning science journalist and widely read columnist for the Hearst newspapers. She is the author of *Drugs and Pain* and *Drugs and Sexual Behavior* in the ENCYCLOPEDIA OF PSYCHOACTIVE DRUGS, published by Chelsea House.

Dale C. Garell, M.D., is medical director of California Children Services, Department of Health Services, County of Los Angeles. He is also associate dean for curriculum at the University of Southern California School of Medicine and clinical professor in the Department of Pediatrics & Family Medicine at the University of Southern California School of Medicine. From 1963 to 1974, he was medical director of the Division of Adolescent Medicine at Children's Hospital in Los Angeles. Dr. Garell has served as president of the Society for Adolescent Medicine, chairman of the youth committee of the American Academy of Pediatrics, and as a forum member of the White House Conference on Children (1970) and White House Conference on Youth (1971). He has also been a member of the editorial board of the *American Journal of Diseases of Children*.

C. Everett Koop, M.D., Sc.D., is Surgeon General, Deputy Assistant Secretary for Health, and Director of the Office of International Health of the U. S. Public Health Service. A pediatric surgeon with an international reputation, he was previously surgeon-in-chief of Children's Hospital of Philadelphia and professor of pediatric surgery and pediatrics at the University of Pennsylvania. Dr. Koop is the author of more than 175 articles and books on the practice of medicine. He has served as surgery editor of the *Journal of Clinical Pediatrics* and editor-in-chief of the *Journal of Pediatric Surgery*. Dr. Koop has received nine honorary degrees and numerous other awards, including the Denis Brown Gold Medal of the British Association of Pediatric Surgeons, the William E. Ladd Gold Medal of the American Academy of Pediatrics, and the Copernicus Medal of the Surgical Society of Poland. He is a Chevalier of the French Legion of Honor and a member of the Royal College of Surgeons, London.